FEELING FASHION

Praise for *Feeling Fashion;*

"Nothing in fashion studies has been done quite like this - you are about to experience a wild, genre-busting ride."
-- Elizabeth Wissinger, Professor of Sociology, CUNY Graduate Center, New York.

~

"Fashion often seems like a mad scramble to decypher obscure and ever-changing rules set by the big brands. Fail to be on trend and the punishment is ridicule. No wonder a lot of people choose to play it safe with their style, and in so doing avoid ridicule but also don't feel much at all about how they appear in the world. Von Busch and Hwang have a different idea, where fashion can be a game played together to stimulate and delight each other through fashion as a social skin. Its an approach to fashion that puts the body and its sensations back in the picture, and even a touch of cognitive and embodied science. All in the name of a better social dynamic."
-- McKenzie Wark, Professor of Culture and Media, The New School, New York.

~

"In *Feeling Fashion,* Otto von Busch and Daye Hwang offer an important, thought-provoking and refreshing contribution to fashion theory by focusing on how fashion triggers our inner desires and bodily passions. They highlight the embodied, sensorial and emotional dimension of fashion, and offer a fruitful theoretical framework to think through and engage with the fashion system in an affirmative and affective way. This focus on actually feeling fashion - physically, biologically, emotionally - and on aesthetic pleasure and play in relation to social dynamics is a very welcome contribution to fashion studies. This helps to move beyond the dominant methodological thread in fashion studies to explore fashion in terms of its textual, linguistic and discursive facets. With their refreshing take, Von Busch and Hwang do more justice to the actual affective relationship between experiential, living bodies and fashion objects."

—- Daniëlle Bruggeman, Professor of Fashion,
ArtEZ University of the Arts , Arnhem.

Authors: Otto von Busch & Daye Hwang

ISBN: 978-91-984047-2-2
New York: SelfPassage 2018

Second edition. with minor corrections (July 2020)
Errors and omissions will be corrected in subsequent editions.

FEELING FASHION

THE EMBODIED GAMBLE OF OUR SOCIAL SKIN

OTTO VON BUSCH & DAYE HWANG

This book came about through a playful mix of ideas and fates. Daye, with a degree in neuroscience from John Hopkins, took one of Otto's courses at Parsons as she was interested in understanding the forces of fashion through experiments in her making practice. At the time, Otto was examining fashion through the lens of psychologist and former New School teacher Wilhelm Reich, and the possibility of thinking fashion as a form of energy in the body. There seemed to be an immediate overlap: perhaps neuroscience and embodiment can reveal new perspectives on how we think of fashion. In many ways, this book is a parallel to *Vital Vogue: A Biosocial Perspective on Fashion*, which takes the passion of flirting as its point of departure. Here, we instead anchor the discussion in the embodied gamble in social relations.

None of us can claim to be an authority on neuroscience, but the basic ideas seemed to excite and make immediate sense to everyone we spoke to. Yet, after discussions with academics, scientists, writers and publishers, we found we had little license to make claims worthy of any weight of proof. With some frustration, we still felt we were onto something, and the more we dug into the theme the more anecdotal data seemed to align with our ideas, and we collected more and more narratives from friends, students, and annotated encounters from Daye's ethnographic research at a second-hand store. So this self-published book is an amalgamation of fashion, gambling and neuroscience, and we make some wild claims. Yet, as a scientist encouraged us along the way: "perhaps you are not right, but it sounds you can be a bit imprecise in an interesting way!"

We want to thank the friends, colleagues and anonymous reviewers who have challenged and helped us develop and articulate these ideas. They know who they are and we are eternally grateful.

CONTENTS

A girl in her teens with blonde hair quickly rushes through the racks, she throws clothes over her arm, racing for first place. She and her mom are from Denver, invited here by a fashion magazine that wishes to collaborate with her on an article.

"My daughter is a style influencer and content creator." She says at the register.

Every item drapes easily over her tall, evenly proportioned body. When she walks out the fitting room, the people in the store don't pretend not to stare. She has a large following on Instagram, but there has lately been some controversies.

"Haters gonna hate," she says, with a worried expression when asked.

Her mother is excited to support her.

"For every new outfit she seems to grow a bit."

....

Almost 70, her moves are soft. She had owned a thrift store
in Baltimore in the 80s so she knows a good deal when she
sees one. Around twice a week, she enters the store to
embark on a personal treasure hunt. She is slow in her
search, with her eye on the details, and quickly passes by the
polyester. Wearing a fitted denim jacket, the seams reversed,
the thread, red; the deconstructed look. Simple black leg-
gings, but fingers adorned with silver rings of many shapes
and sizes. Each seam makes sharp her petite, fragile, hunched
body.

"You need to be bold to wear hats." She wears hers with a
silver pin.

She picks out a bright purple lambswool with a thick, navy
blue border around the edge, made in Italy. It engulfs the
whole of her head for just $5.

Now just a finishing touch of fresh lipstick.

. . . .

She is an emerging designer at a reception, wearing a new Zendaya bodysuit she has not worn before, but she loves its sheer fabric and deep cut. As she moves between groups of people, an editor of some esteem is talking to a group of artists she recognizes from the West Coast. She approaches the group, and the editor looks at her from top to bottom, finishing with just the smallest hint of rolling her eyes.

"What are you wearing?"

The editor's voice is just slightly louder than conversation tone, yet with an intonation making it obvious there is answer expected. One in the group sniggers, but with seeming awkwardness.

Two years later, the designer shares the story with us.

"You know, I am grown up, but at that moment I just felt so embarrassed I wanted to go home and change, even though I had just felt great just minutes before."

The memory still occupies her.

"Some nights, it keeps me awake, thinking about how I should have replied her in some smart way that didn't make me feel like a fool. Its weird, I keep replaying the scene in my head, thinking what I should have done. I mean, basically, the way she said it, it felt like she just undressed me in front the others."

INTRODUCTION

Our everyday encounters with fashion can be quite mundane, as the short snippets intersecting this book show.[1] In their quotidian tone they reveal some basic yet essential aspects of everyday dress which interest us: that what many of us consider being "fashion" is an adventurous play and a gamble of sorts. In contrast to the kinds of fashion we meet on the catwalks or in the mainstreet stores, it seems these people are not seeking confirmation of trends, or a cheap cure to low blood sugar with an easily accessible piece of clothing. Instead they are seeking something else; an excitement, a moment of risk taking, a form of sartorial thrill, something like a dopamine kick, a rushing sense of aliveness.[2]

Not all fashion experiences are such thrill, and we don't always gamble.[3] Sometimes we just want to blend in, we play it safe. Some days we modulate the play, covering up a dress with a trench-coat on public transport, to later, at the nightclub, reveal it. Or simply add some make-up just before it is time to play. Articulating an approach to fashion based on gambling is novel to us, while it also seems intuitive. Many people we have encountered confirm its basic premise: the "passion" of fashion is a sort of social play, a gamble, a thrill felt in the body as we test our look against the attention of our peers - does it work or not, do we sense affirmation or subtle snubs? Fashion is a desire, an energy, a social challenge that we feel like a rush through the body. If we were to see fashion from the body, what would we see? Or perhaps more accurately: *what would we feel?*[4]

Throughout this text, we as authors use a generous "we" to engage the reader to unpack fashion with us. We are all somehow engaged in fashion, whether we think of it or not, or want it or not, and all cultures engage in the modification of looks.[5] Yet it is also important to acknowledge play is not equally distributed. The possibility to engage in fashion differs radically between abilities, attitudes, privilege and items of dress. Some can always play an upper hand, while some play a totally different game.[6] But since our intention is to frame fashion as a feeling, and more specifically a feeling of gambling, rather than only what is seen in the stores, we open for a more inclusive "we" to understand the play of fashion.

The argument of this book is that fashion acts simultaneously as a prosthesis of the imagination and a physical extension of the body.[7] Clothes are not only an intimate, constant part of our environment, but, like our skin, they are active and busy extensions of our sensory organs, creators of our lived environments. As social and physical prosthetics, clothes orient our intentional perceptions via our emotions to the extent that they can be considered extensions of our embodied minds. Clothes, rather than being disconnected or dismissible as rational/irrational adornment as argued in the general discourse around fashion, are cognitive prosthetics.[8]

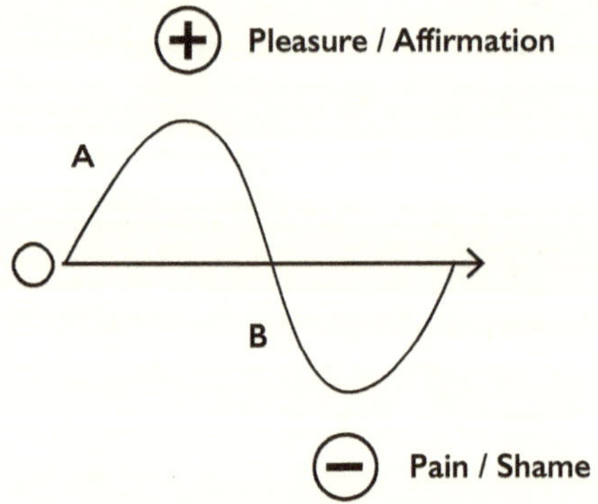

Fashion gambling/risk-taking
(A) Adoption, positive valance, (B) failure, negative valance

We use these prosthetics to sense our world, and we do this through play. As opposed to clothing, fashion is an emotional *gamble*. If I wear fashion I put myself out to *be judged by others*, and either this emotional gamble works or it does not. I seek aesthetic judgment, and I try to present my case in the most rewarding way: sexually, culturally, subculturally, economically, whichever currency I have and arena I wish to gamble on. Or I can seek the exuberant, attainable only to the selected few, the richest, in the quest for what fashion theorist Rebecca Arnold calls the "thrill of exclusion."[9]

For something to be working "fashionably" it needs to be putting some social currency at risk, in exchange for the opportunity to raise our social status or undermine it: we are either rewarded or punished, and if we sought attention, being ignored may be experienced as a failure.[10] But the humiliation that may come from losing can also be traumatic, and we may withdraw from the game to stay safe in conformity, in the plain uniforms which offer neither risk nor reward.[11] But the game is more complex than that: a professional may stay within accepted boundaries, using subtle details to place our bets in the game, such as subtly colored socks or a daring tie, while a hipster may back up a daring statement with an "ironic" detail in order save a path of retreat if the gamble fails.

In his classic work, cultural theorist Johan Huizinga places play as a basic element of human culture.[12] To Huizinga, "play" is more than games. It is a principle of culture's creative quality and a spirit of togetherness. It is a free activity, with its own boundaries, standing outside everyday life. Play is as much about fantasy as discipline, and it is illusive, manageable risk-taking. It creates an order outside "real" life, while at the same time enacting an almost absolute freedom in that sphere. It allows experimental cultures and relationships to form and develop.[13] To Huizinga, games are not the residue of culture, but a part of its essence, and to fully understand culture we must also examine its elements of play.

While Huizinga emphasises the tensions between freedom, fantasy, contest and discipline in play, Roger Caillois produces a typology to unpack with what logics play and games operate in human relationships. On the one hand, play contains elements of calculation and submission to rules and order, that Caillois calls *ludus*, and on the other hand, it also comprises of the free, spontaneous, tumultuous, active and exuberant, that he calls *paidia*.[14] Within its boundaries, play is ephemeral and sources its energy from the passions. It is "a waste of time, energy, ingenuity, skill, and often of money".[15]

Interestingly, Caillois sets the mask, and the play with identity, as one of play's fundamental elements, "a sacred object universally present, whose transformation into a plaything perhaps marks a prime mutation in the history of civilization."[16] The mask supports make-believe, it is amorous as well as a symbol of political intrigue. It protects and liberates, and creates an awareness of a second reality or of a free unreality, in an asymmetrical relationship to social conventions. Pretend-play, secrecy and transposition of roles into representation and the imaginary are essential to play; it is an essential displacement of the self into the sphere of the game where the outcome is put to risk.[17]

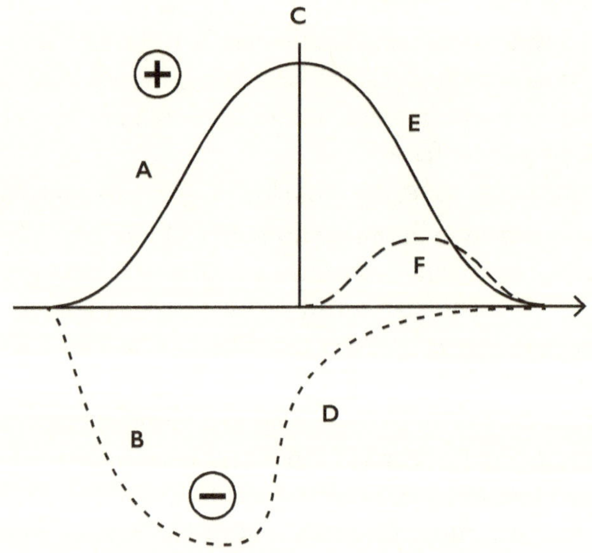

Fashion risk placed in trend curve
(A) early adoption, higher risk/reward, (B) higher risk of failure in
testing new trend, (C) trend peak, (D) steep decline in risk at trend
peak, (E) safe play and declining reward as trend ebbs,
(F) dead zone - minimal reward as trend ends

The power of fashion is spread through media: the markers of the game come from the fashion system. When music artist Cardi B wears a certain Gucci bag, it is imbued with a magic that makes it irresistible to her fans and those who are invested in following her. Soon we start to see it in the hallway, on the street, and we begin to imagine what it would look like on our bodies as we sense amongst our peers and co-players that anything Cardi B has is high currency in the game at this moment. Through the peer-validation of the Cardi B image, the positive emotions we have towards Cardi B are amplified through our daily interactions amongst our peers. This gets transferred onto the clothing through non-conscious mechanisms and makes an Instagram user spend time and money they don't have. All of this is transferred through emotional systems that drive behavior without our conscious awareness. An interaction that happens, in its most powerful form, through our emotions in everyday life, on the streets and in the hallways.[18]

Fashion is a way to play socially with emotions. It can upset as well as manifest social positions, relationships, loyalties, aspirations and desires. With its mimetic and agonistic elements, it allows for various levels of risk-taking, while simultaneously leaving room for pretend-play.[19] As we gamble with our clothes, putting ourselves out there to be judged, we learn to play more skillfully, which can translate to evolving a strategy for playing well, or a "style" of dress, a set of masks, markers and play tokens, but also invitations and seduction to play together.[20] This can be a mix of our own initiatives and risks, as well as more rule-abiding sets following explicit guidance from brands and stylists. We learn to read social settings, what is expected and how much room there is for play and deviance, while unpacking the dynamics of peer expectations and interactions.[21]

The experience of fashion often overlaps the experience of shopping fashion; both are often a social experience, and part of the shopping thrill is trying things on and playing with several outfits and combinations in the mirror. Shopping is an integral part of the pretend-play, the imaginative projection of oneself in a new skin or new setting, the formation and preparation for the gamble. This is often heightened in the interplay with an accompanying friend, acting as a juror: "Is this me?" But also the play with other shoppers (what are they getting? I saw that first!), and the interaction with shop-attendants is part of building the feelings we have for garments. The thrill of shopping fashion is also the therapeutic pleasure, knowing the new purchase can immediately be worn. It is a new skin: I can walk out of the store in my new shoes, playing my new self.

Economist John Howard, for example, argues that shopping can indeed be seen as a form of therapeutic play in Huizinga's sense of the word, and highlights how shopping ties into play's three central characteristics; freedom, elusiveness and boundedness. Free and super-fluous, shopping as therapy engages in voluntary, "fun," yet still plays with rebelliousness and the tensions between conformity and non-conformity, as it often builds on an illusive distinction from "ordinary life."

> "While shopping's freedom from ordinary externally imposed rules symbolically removes it from that world, shopping is further distanced in that it allows respondents to choose the rules by which they shop. These shopping rules vary among individuals, but there are certain categories of rules that apply to all respondents. These categories are concerned with managing spending, shopping procedure, and solitude."[22]

As Howard emphasizes, risk is an important part of the thrill of playful shopping, "Because of its makebelieve nature, however, the thrill of play is experienced as excitement rather than as the anxiety that results from risk in the ordinary world." Howard further points out how such dangerous play is an example of what Clifford Geertz calls "deep play," characterized by rebelliousness and risk.[23] Like play, shopping is also guided by implicit rules, codes and price tags. While each shopping routine may be unique, shoppers often have their own formal template of values and activity. In Howard's study, Elizabeth, a PhD student, for example, called her shopping "ritualistic" and "formalized," while Marcy, inspects everything in the stores she patronizes: "Stay, as much as you can, intense about it... I hit the whole store, and I do touch every corner. I look at everything."[24]

According to Howard, in shopping people can rebel against productive stress to concentrate on their enjoyment in playful risk. Feeling in control while still on adventure. "Hunting" for something new, mixing pretend play with the physical experience of taking home the outcome of the adventure. As a respondent posits, getting the "adrenaline going" when she decides to "whip out a couple of hundred dollars."[25]

However, as Caillois warns, games are continually corrupted to become absorbed into real life, to become reified into labor and made into a living, thus losing their passion and power of recreation. It becomes a work, a necessity, a constant activity and absorbed into everyday struggles for subsistence.[26] In a similar vein, we may become aversive to the playfulness of fashion, fearful of the risks, and drawn into habitual or anxious patterns of stress and retreating to the safest and lowest denominator, refusing to play.

Yet still the game goes on, the judgments are still made. As the self is not a fixed essence, clothes play a role in our constantly reconstructed, multi-layered sense of self, and this process also includes risk-taking, play and gambling. Specifically, clothes guide the construction of self by providing feedback that we process through our emotions, in continuous interaction with our surroundings, through play, pretend, mimesis and competition. Our self-image is a *dressed self-image*. The image is not passive, but actively seeking out responses from the surroundings. We feel both attraction and rejection, desire and shame through the way we wear clothes. By gambling, we *feel* the way clothing works or fails in our spine as much as in the head, and this emotional "feel" for our social environment guides the development of the different layers of self. We claim that our ideal selves, the person we imagine ourselves to be, the dressed self that received the most positive reviews, the feeling of being Cardi that I experience when I wear her clothes, exists as a set of neural patterns. It is an affectively charged image that we would like to call a "ghost-image" or a "fashion phantom".

This fashion phantom and ghost create conditions for desire, between a material reality and a sensed, desirable state, not unlike a phantom limb. As with the phantom limb, this ghost image is rooted in a continuous sense of amputation: a void between our embodied selves and the image and character of who we wish to be (or be seen as). The void fuels our desires to change and edit our sense of self, to seek new prosthetics to fill the self-image with confidence. As we gamble with fashion, the garments fill this aesthetic and emotional void in an ephemeral way, acting as a prosthesis that empowers our amputated sense of self. We feel more whole as we play and engage with the prosthetics that connect our desires with our lived experience.

As we practice walking in high heels, we gain not only posture, but confidence, a new stride, a new behavior, a new self-esteem. And not unlike a dancer we can train our ability and proprioception to better feel the position, place, motion and emotion of our body.[27] The right pair of heels enhances the power of both appearance and our sense of being,[28] perhaps not unlike when riding a motorcycle, attention to the world takes a new shape; a "material reflection of a spiritual reality," as Robert Pirsig explained the magic of motorcycles in his famous *Zen and the Art of Motorcycle Maintenance*.[29] Heels, or other garments, can be a vehicle for our embodiment and bring about a similar "spiritual reality." In addition to engaging with garments as tangible prosthetics which shape our bodies and sensorium, they also exist as images which inform our desires and ideals of who we are and could be: our present and ideal self. And while it may seem unromantic, our emotions are essentially the mechanism we use to survive in the world. Our emotional infrastructure helps us judge something's value. Indeed, reason is not devoid of emotion but rather dependent on it.[30]

Throughout this work, we define clothes as physical garments, whereas fashion has a metaphysical quality added onto clothing, connected to the social imagination. The distinction is not clear cut, but on a grade of intensity: some clothes also have an intensity of collective desires imagined around them. Yet, as all clothes are steeped in the time of their making, and thus related to the realm of fashion, they are not untouched by fashion. Even outfits we see as "timeless" signify the collective imaginations of their time, such as coronation or religious dress.[31] But more importantly, whereas all clothes are physical extensions of the sensory body, fashion also connects to a special collective imagination of prestige, adoration, desire. These two concepts exist on a continuum rather than as two distinct definitions. On the one end, we place clothes as physical and material extensions of our bodies, and manifestations of our needs. On the other end, fashion is an extended prosthesis of the self, and ties to a collectively produced temporal and ephemeral fantasy world of desire, filling the void of our imperfectness. Along this continuum, clothes of various sorts and desires are various physical prostheses to an individual's sense of prestige, adoration, desire, where fashion speaks of the *competitive* desires of a specific time and community where the wearer can fulfil a better, higher-performing, more-attractive and successful me.[32] A garment like a short red dress may play with desires and fantasies, and in that way be social, but a popular fashion also plays with prestige in time for a group of people, and is part of a popular social gamble: who is "in" and who is "out?"

Or to put it differently, clothes are the textile "hardware" of dress, and fashion is a "software" of dreams, a looping program "running" on top of this textile hardware, tying together our body with the shared dreams, fantasies and *phantasma,* the mental images or apparitions of a certain Zeitgeist. With practice, we can develop the sensorium towards the ephemeral aesthetics of fashion, making us able to *touch and feel the shared desires of our time.* We use each term when we point towards a situation closer to one of the poles: clothes closer to the "hardware," fashion closer to the "software."

So if fashion is a "spiritual reality" or a software operating through feelings in the body, we use it to play in this shared world, and we experience its intensity in our bodies through social bets in an aesthetic gamble. We play with prestige and reputation, and bet with the possibility of humiliation. It can be a high stake gamble. Yet, to engage in fashion is to go for a quotidian adventure, challenge the world for a small quake of the soul, a passion we cannot fully experience in social isolation; what a lovely game to play.

. . . .

A young Latina woman, around 25, with a round face and a quick step walks into the store with furrowed brows.

"I'm looking for something nice. I have a date tomorrow after work, so I need something formal that doesn't make me stand out at work, but also looks nice."

She wears a black skirt that hits her at her knees, pants, form-filling, dark blazers to work, sometimes with a pop of color. Body hugging lace, spandex, and corset-y clothes. Not too revealing, not too much. The harder to zip up, the more she loves them. The body presses tightly against her vision of sexy.

She picks items off the rack that are foreign to her... anything from a red chinese traditional top (qípáo), a peruvian poncho with green and blue stripes, to an intricately embroidered striped purple Indian tunic... and all the variations of new in between.

In the tail end of a break up, she had left her clothes at his house and while she had some cheap clothes to last her for a couple weeks, they served as poignant reminders to her of that night. She missed her old clothes but couldn't have them back. She didn't want them back, it'd be too painful.

So she found herself thrifting, trying to find a silhouette, a texture, a color, something from somewhere else that she did not know. Something that could bring more life than she was feeling at the moment.

"I need empathy training."

A young man of fair complexion blushes. One can tell he is one of the popular guys. He tells about his teenage blog, with its explicit "do" and "don't" section. It started out as a joke, but it needed to be kept active, otherwise it was not there. He felt compelled to seek out something to post.

"I took a picture of a girl whose butt was hanging out of her shorts, and called it a 'don't.'"

They were not so many degrees apart as he first thought, just in another class. She found it and wrote him back. He cringes as he tells the story.

"I'm an asshole."

It is no coincidence clothing is often referred to as a "second skin," not only because it sits on top of the skin, but because it is a skin in a very literal way: it may extend from our flesh, but is still part of our body.[33] Anthropologist Terence Turner points out that textiles and clothing are essential parts of our social reality. To Turner, the "social skin" of the body, our clothes, are part of a socio-symbolic dimension of our sociality, they are part of our social as much as our physical survival. Clothing enacts our social standing and the roles we distribute throughout our shared world and thus marks off our relation to others; social status, territory, gender, profession and age.[34] With the social skin, every bodily accentuation signifies social meaning in correspondence with the sociocultural context. As Turner suggests, clothing is, similar to religion, a serious matter.[35]

Thinking clothing as a social "skin" may risk rendering clothing as less active, as we tend to consider skin a stable, static, protective membrane. However, recent studies show that the sensations felt through our skin, largely operating in the unconscious, are powerful determinants of thoughts and behavior, and thus vital to our survival.[36]

Clothes add a layer onto our bodies, modulating our sensorial world. The extra layer amplifies our body, protects it, but also extrudes from it. This added skin allows us to play with danger: we can modulate temperatures, walk on sharp pebbles, move comfortably through thorny bushes, survive in hostile atmospheres. Clothes make us superhuman: they allow us to take risks. With their power, our sensations of the environment changes. When we're wearing gloves, we know where our fingers end and the gloves begin, our motor skills quickly adapt to their new bulky grip. We can take the gloves off and leave them on the counter; they are a second skin, but simultaneously not.

When finding a glove that fits your hand perfectly, it protects the hand while also transforming your hand into a sensual tool. It's skin molds to every bump and crevice, and you may choose to wear the gloves even if the weather does not necessarily force you to do so. The glove becomes part of you in a very special way. While it may serve a very physical function, protecting the hand, you may also feel pride and pleasure, attracting your own as well as the attention of others. Those pleasing leather gloves fit you in two very distinct ways, onto your physical body and into a better concept of yourself: the gloves help you touch risks as well as desires.[37] If we define our cognition as contingent with its material extensions and context, the body morphs into an amalgamation, or an assemblage, with clothing: where exactly do our bodies end and our clothes begin?[38]

Without the support of our extra layer of protection, our living environment could be anxiety inducing; the extra "skin" of clothes help us navigate the risks of physical as well as social environments. It thus makes sense to take a closer look at the skin, the largest organ of the body and a direct surface of interaction with clothes.

Our haptic intelligence is vital to our human intelligence, that is, our sense of touch and embodiment ties directly into our conceptions and thinking: it's just that we don't notice it. According to American writer Adam Gopnik, "touch is the unsung sense - the one that we depend on most and talk about least...we are so used to living within our skins that we allow them to introduce themselves as neutral envelopes, capable of excitation at the extremities (and at extreme movements), rather than as busy, body-sensing organs."[39] Indeed, our skin contains an extensive network of specific nerve endings and touch receptors known as the somatosensory system[40] that give rise to pressure, vibrations, stretch, texture, temperature, and pain. While extreme, perceivable sensations lead to action (i.e. when you touch a hot stove) even subtle, imperceptible sensations have an impact on our emotions, where the skin acts as transductor.

Studies show that people who held something warm were more likely to perceive others as emotionally warm and to be kind, friendly and generous.[41] Similarly, body posture and movements have, in some experiments, shown to unconsciously affect thoughts and behaviors.[42] Clothing interacts directly with skin and is a major determinant of the movement and postures of the body. If holding a warm cup induces warmer behaviors, how might a soft silk or a tough denim affect our behaviors? Additionally, would the extra height of high heels result in authoritative behaviors or a wider silhouette allow for freer thought? If the skin is such a rich sensory organ, should not clothes also affect our cognition?

Our senses are not passive, but rather primed as seekers; they stretch out to touch their sensory environment, continuously seeking clues of what's going on. They are "enactive"[43] as well as "embodied" in the way that our thinking and our bodies are inextricably linked in the sense that our minds are grounded in a bodily experience, in a way similar to the Greek idea of *episteme* (knowledge) bound *phantasia* to *aesthesis* (sensation).[44] The kind of thinking that emerges from these systems, consistent with the way our body works, takes place at unconscious and non-linguistic levels.[45]

The idea of embodiment stands in direct contrast to the postulations of Rene Descartes, who wrote in the 17th century that the mind is entirely different from the body: the brain houses the soul of man while the body is merely a machine controlled by the mind, and there is a distinct border between the two. It also diverges from the cognitive science movement, which used a computer as it's model for the brain, and thus viewed it as an information processing machine that makes rational choices for its survival using algorithms and symbols that are represented as neural patterns. Embodied cognition, on the other hand, posits that the mind is not only connected to the body, but that the very process of cognition arises from the physical nature of our brains, bodies, and bodily experiences. We *are in our senses*, in our milieu of cognitive mechanisms.[46] As Maurice Merleau-Ponty posits, we are simultaneously subject and object to ourselves, that is, being means *being inseparably in a body*, not merely a disconnected soul "driving" a body: our very selfhood is located in the body.[47]

The philosophical ideas of embodiment gained steam with discoveries in neuroscience at the end of the 20th century. One major finding was that a person viewing others move activated the same areas in the brain that would be activated if the viewer were carrying out that action: if I see you eat a banana it will activate the same areas of the brain as if I ate it myself. The specific brain response was activity in the premotor cortex (the area of the brain that gives rise to motor activity) and the specific type of neurons were deemed "mirror neurons." This suggests that instead of representing information as symbols that are processed in our minds, we gain knowledge of another person's experience through "passive" re-experiencing of the action in direct correspondence with our own body. Our bodies are thus wired neurally to be social: we can "feel" each other in a very tangible way, not reliant on the semiotic coding and decoding of messages.[48] We are wired mimetically.

On a basic level, if I look more professional, people will treat me differently, making me behave more professionally, and they will also judge my performance as better.[49] Some psychological studies have shown how people wearing different clothes can alter the wearer's judgment and behaviors and assume certain roles and identities. Certain garments do change our perception of both the world and ourselves. A person may behave differently towards others if he or she wears an explicit name-tag versus an anonymous balaclava, or if wearing a uniform.[50] Also, feeling exposed may make us shy, just like feeling safe and protected may make us more expressive.[51] Power dressing should thus not only be understood as a form of social symbolism, but as a real emotion on the body of the wearer: it builds superpowers, allowing the wearer to bet higher in the gamble.[52]

But the opposite is also true, that emotions are enclothed in vulnerability, which may suggest weakness or provoke humiliation, and many social rituals play explicitly with these emotions. Take for example hazing, which is usually a socially accepted form of psychological torture of various degrees. A central component of such rite of passage is usually to make the newcomers feel exposed and submissive, inflicting pain through derision, and where the subject is often dressed in some ridiculous outfit and pushed to perform outrageous behavior as a step towards becoming accepted, or initiated into a group.[53]

Hajo Adam and Adam Galinsky's idea of "enclothed cognition" pins down an embodied perspective on clothing to highlight how clothes influence the wearer's psychological processes and behavioral tendencies. The clothing we wear plays an integral part of how we perceive and behave in the world.[54] Simply put, I modulate my psychological and bodily attention and behavior depending on what I wear. In their study, Adam and Galinsky found that wearing a lab coat changed the perception and behavior of the participants in a lab. The coat, signifying a certain clinical practice and scientific focus with its emphasis on being careful and paying attention to the task at hand, added to their performance in increased sustained attention.[55]

> "when a piece of clothing is worn, it exerts an influence on the wearer's psychological processes by activating associated abstract concepts through its symbolic meaning—similar to the way in which a physical experience, which is, by definition, already embodied, exerts its influence."[56]

The garment is thus a *cognitive extension of our skin*, an *emotional prosthetic*,[57] which connects the social world "out there" to our emotions and psychological functions, modulating our embodiment with the symbolic status and meanings of garments, and our feelings in fashion plays on such perceptive transformations.[58] Clothes orient the cognition of both the wearers as well as the audience. For example, as we dress up for a night out we attune our dress from the perhaps formal work wear to something "appropriate," something that balances expected risk and reward, of the setting we plan to visit.[59]

When we dress up, we *orient* ourselves towards a task or a meeting, to the risk and reward of a coming cognitive situation. Like the young Latina woman in the opening snippet, she claims she feels attractive in the tightly zipped garments; they hold her up, while also fitting tightly around her idea of sexiness. The fit and tactility of the garments situate her experience, and she may choose carefully when to use these garments and in what context. In this sense, the seductive part of fashion is part of an enclothed cognition: if the garment is considered hot I will also feel hotter in it - and act as if I am hot and with a seductive sense of self.[60]

With clothes, we touch the world of dressed sociality through play and risk-taking; we test boundaries, feel out the forms of social life and identity, sense the possibilities of how we can drape and give expression to the many aspects and aspirations of identity, use clothes to connect to others, gain influence, and get what we want. We train the image that guides our usage of the "stick" of our sensorium, the feedback we get in return updates the image. The final objective is to successfully navigate through our everyday environment.

Fashion, the superhuman prosthetic

Clothing is a prosthetic for the body, an extended skin. The term prosthetics usually signifies an artificial component replacing a missing or dismembered limb, filling in a lack to restore the body in order to meet everyday challenges. Some prosthetics, such as eyeglasses, were not too long ago reserved for medical purposes but have moved into the realm of everyday aesthetics and to the heart of fashion. Hipsters can be seen wearing glassless frames just to add a distinguishing feature to the face while for the general public sunglasses are now a prerequisite of the cool summer look, meeting the everyday challenge of the social status games.

In a more general sense, prosthetics enhance the body of its wearer in some way, and not necessarily only to the standard of "normal" function.[61] The popular enhancements offered by prosthetics have pushed the boundaries of the normative realm of beauty. Only a generation ago, braces were a terror for teens with severe problems with their teeth, but they have now, especially in the US, become almost a rite of passage to guarantee a future perfect smile. The boundaries for the normative body are continually pushed forward and to higher required standards for what is considered "acceptable," and in some senses, beyond the acceptable towards the super-human.[62]

It is worth noticing that on a technical level, clothing prosthetics have improved immensely over the last decades, from synthetic blends and stretch materials to rain clothes and athletic sports clothes. A famous example can be the banned "shark-skin" swim suits which over a year improved several world records. Similarly, high performance outdoor materials are today used in much everyday clothing.

However, bodies are amplified as well as maimed by prosthetics as these amplifications work in relation to societal constructions of abilities and what is expected of a fully productive body. Societal norms define which bodies are not whole, which are often aged, raced, gendered, classed bodies. As we will point to later on, the fashion prosthesis enable us to feel a world of desires, but it also just barely fills a gap of craving which feeds into a continuous sense of deficiency: *it creates a need*.[63] What is culturally considered a "fully functional body" is always in flux and often less reliant on medical technologies as much as on commodities.

From a perspective of embodiment, prosthetics are not mere fill-ins in a situation of dismemberment, but a process which transforms both body and mind, they have a deeply immersive dimension.[64] As sociologist Cassandra Crawford adds, prosthetics are alloplastic extensions of the mind, inhabited by the body of the user, as they "bruise, rub, lacerate, and fatigue, while also being 'worn in' and lived-as-flesh."[65] A prosthetic becomes for the user a "companion technology" and fuses with the body because of nature's malleability. Eyeglasses are a very quotidian example where users do not recognize wearing them (even if wearing in a new pair can be painful for the skin on the nose). Effective prosthetics have a high level of "taken-for-grantedness" as they interface deeply and indelibly with the nerves and muscles of the user's body.[66] The neuronal malleability between prosthesis and phantom limbs has triggered great interest from neuroscientists as this relation opens an unexpected window to study the relations between body and brain.[67] In similar ways, clothes are prosthetics: they enhance our capacity to sense and act in a "taken-for-granted" way.[68]

In its most direct sense, the texture of fabrics adds a specific type of sensibility to the skin. Some types of light fabrics, silk for example, add a light and feather-like touch across the skin, almost like a tickle. In other cases I come to sense the humidity of the weather as the moist fabric sticks to my skin in a way I would not necessarily experience with my skin bare. When it comes to actions, the prosthetic can be a pair of boots, which armor my feet, enhancing my ability to walk over rough terrain or in wet conditions for longer distances. Or pockets that enable me to carry and organize the objects I want to carry with me, such as the workman's pants.[69]

From an aesthetic perspective, history is full of examples of bodily enhancements, from the minor involvements of jewelry and make-up to scarification and body modifications. Other types of prosthetics extend the very boundaries and constitutions of my body. As we perceive the world, we usually come to think of our surrounding world as objects and ourselves as subjects. We see ourselves as the agents of the world, while objects are outside of us. But, as Merleau-Ponty suggests, when I use one hand to grab my other arm, I turn my arm into an object for my grasp.[70] The distinctions between who is subject and who is object are in flux and often intermingle, if they even can be differentiated at all.[71] A more explicit example is the blind man's stick that extends the sensing body of the user: the hand stretches out to "feel" the world, transmitting the resistant force of obstacles as it touches them. But we could think of prosthetics as much more immaterial and obtuse, while also much more social than primarily individual extensions between body and environment.

Similarly, we unconsciously *feel* when we are seen.[72] Our attention is drawn to the gaze of others (and sometimes we have to fight the reflex of looking back). We become conscious of people looking at us even in the periphery of our visual field.[73] And a child quickly gets continuously attentive to the perception of the parents, when they are looking or not, and often calls on attention in order to affirm that they matter ("look mom, no hands!").[74]

On a more symbolic level we often think of clothing as a communicative prosthesis: that it reaches out to touch others *for* us. I wear a garment to mark and manifest an affiliation, a community or a standpoint. Clothes are often more discreet than language and do not necessarily translate or need to be "reasonable." At a hospital it is a great advantage if doctors wear special coats so the patient does not have to ask every person if he or she is the doctor they should speak to. In that way, clothes can signal certain expectations towards capabilities or actions. But the opposite may also occur, that is, the prosthesis *delegates* action from the fleshy body towards the prosthesis itself. Psychologist Robert Pfaller argues that technologies do not necessarily make us more interactive, but he instead means many gadgets produce a certain form of delegation of behavior he calls "interpassivity."[75] We may think we are very interactive, that we engage intensely with our surrounding, but as Pfaller argues, we simply shift our attention and let our surroundings guide us by cues or nudges. For example, canned laughter in TV shows not only tells me when to laugh, but it also makes me feel I have company and enjoy the show together with others. In its extreme, the TV laughs instead of me.

In a similar vein, certain garments make me ready to act, indeed make me feel like I am *going* to act, or even replace my actions all together. I buy some cool active sports gear, so I look like I am ready for a tough survival trek, even though I live in town and drive everywhere. Or in another case I get myself some yoga-wear, even though I am not on my way to the studio, yet the smooth and stretchy fit of the garments make me feel more agile and at-home-in-the-world. I may have extended my experience of the yoga studio into my daily environment and in the end actually replace my time doing real sun-salutations.

Most of our lifestyle garments are communicated and sold to us in this way: even if you are not really part of the punk, skate, surfer or outdoor sports scene, at least you can feel like you are part of the active community. The brand offers you the commodity, which replicates the "codes" of the scene into a pre-packaged format to be sold as ready-to-wear.[76] Another more common example is how many of us buy smaller clothing to spur our desire to lose weight, our "optimistic clothes" that often hang in the wardrobe as some form of hopeful tokens, yet seldom manage to motivate any change in our eating or exercise regimens. If translated to the realm of language, interpassivity is "much talk and no action."[77]

But we can also think of prosthetics that transforms us both in a cognitive sense as well as socially. An example can be sunglasses. Cass Frankenstein, interviewed by Hanna Rosin and Alix Spiegel, is an interesting case of a man who was bullied as a child for his glasses, and came to rely on prescription sunglasses to the extent that today as an adult, he wears them everywhere.[78] He describes his first time walking into school with the tinted glasses on as if he was "like a ghost almost… like people did not really notice [him], […] as if he were look[ing] at the world through a telescope or from behind a wall." He confesses "when I try to look at people when I speak, I get kind of flustered if I'm not wearing the glasses, and I don't know exactly what to say. It's 'cause of, you know, my shield is down. So it's a matter of their comfort or my comfort." When during the interview, he takes off his glasses and "suddenly, there was a transformation.…The man, who just a moment ago was so sure of himself, now looked naked and vulnerable. Even his voice had changed." After putting his glasses back on, once again, he changed back to his sunglassed self, back to cracking jokes, dancing, even singing.

On a more physical level clothes act as prosthetics as they empower and prepare us for certain action and on a very practical level facilitate such action. In the case of practical dress, a woman working as carpenter has her workwear outfit on, with its rough canvas fabrics, tough seams and all its pockets for tools. Not only can she find all these tools without looking; she knows, almost by reflex, where to reach for the hammer or more nails, but the outfit also attunes her cognition to "think" like a carpenter: she sees details that need adjustment, a nail sticking out from the floor boards, etc. She is ready to be active in the world, and the garments align her towards that type of attention.[79] By channeling the possessive power of her prosthetic attire she has added the possibility to *possess* her environment, and through her extended sensibility she can do so.

The prosthesis can also act on the level of social cognition, of how we perceive, understand and "feel each other out" using clothes as a mode to attune sensibilities, attitudes, attention and orientations. For example, this evening our model carpenter dresses up for a night out, which may attune her dress for another type of attention than her usual work-attire. Indeed, she may be "tuning in" the attention she gives to her look so that the expression of her body enhancements attune to the attention from a possible partner.

It is in the preparation to dress up for a night out we may encounter many aspects of how dress works to enhance our embodied cognition. Our model has gotten to know from experience (from comments from friends and glances from people she would like to impress) how some clothes are attuned or oriented towards the attention of peers.[80] Some garments are "programmed" to meet certain attention, often falling into stereotypical behaviours, but also enhancing certain forms of embodied cognition, such as a professional suit, a sports outfit, a sexy dress.[81] Indeed, the feedback-loop from the embodied cognition may reaffirm the workings of the garment: I feel professional in this suit - people treat me more professionally - I feel even more professional in the suit.

In a similar vein, our model may decide to wear a pair of high heels tonight, not only gaining a higher ground, embodying the cognition of "gaining a few inches," but also making her feel it is a special evening. She attunes her attention to be more social and festive, leaving carpentry problems and introversion behind, and the prosthetics act on her cognition to do just so. She is ready to be seen. She may even add another layer of prosthetics to her experience: before going out, she takes a selfie of herself in the mirror and posts online, exposing her best self (not really retouched, but she had to take a few trials to get the posture and light right) - this is an image of her public persona and the self she wants to present tonight. With this photo she is proud of her looks and feels on top of herself, empowered by her prosthetics.[82] She is ready to possess her social environment and grab some attention.

Grabbing attention

When we say a garment can "grab" someone's attention, this should be taken literally. Attention can be grabbed through dress because we can use clothes skillfully as a sensory organ to touch the senses of others. If we imagine an observer looking and vision stretching out like a limb, feeling around for a special sensory signal, our clothes are another limb, stretching out to "greet" the attentive limb of the other. If what I wear matches what the other sensory limb is looking for, I may grab it and hold it. So when we "catch" someone's attention, we seize it in its drifting and often subconscious path. "Holding" someone's attention is a literal action!

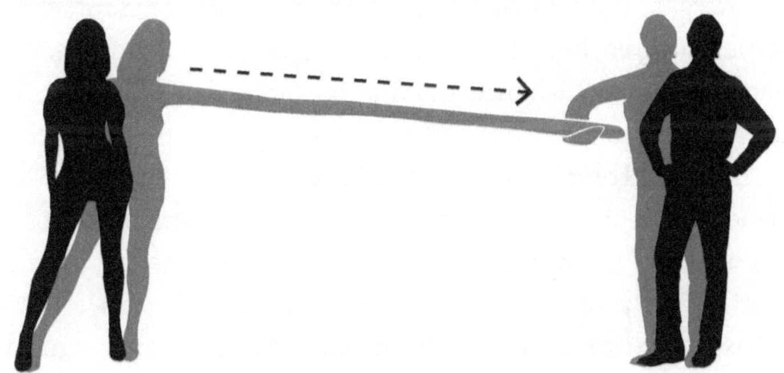

Our attention is like tentacles, reaching across the environment, feeling for markers and cues. When we "grab someone's attention" our attention literally catches their senses, holding their attention.

As our attention is out touching around the environment we seek signals we can register. Signals from the environment are loaded with emotional cues and somatic markers; I see a snack bar and my impression is charged with pleasure. Or I see something disgusting and sicken. For fashion we seek similar perceptual keys: they catch our attention. Like perfume, we cannot ignore it, it sneaks upon us.

For example, the new branded shoes are creating the new buzz this season, in this case let's call the brand GARAP.[83] They are slightly mysterious, only available to the selected few, yet "everybody" seems to talk about them. The shoes do not have the logo written all over them, and are just a little different from the other shoes out there, but just that little difference makes them a lot more attractive. I have encountered the branded shoe, have seen the ads and looked them up online, and the brand objects have implanted themselves as images in my mind: GARAP. Now, unconsciously, my perception is searching for branded cues, the mystery has awoken my attention for this little difference. I may not pay full attention to the street as I am out walking, but suddenly my vision is drawn to the feet of one of the cool kids at school, and I suddenly recognize a matching perceptual key: the GARAP shoes! My attention and desire have been mutually enhanced and the brand now has a place in my mind. Like a mild form of schizophrenia I start seeing the brand everywhere, not unlike a spy feeling followed by agents.

A similar evolution happens in our sensibilities when a new trend emerges. First most of us don't really recognize it until it's on celebrities and reaches our instagram feeds. These symbols, carried by aesthetic images and algorithms that haunt our social media feeds, enter the ads on our facebooks page and into the shops we frequent. By this point, our attention has grasped it and produced a "key" for seeing it. The key is an image, a schema, or an emotional map that has made its way into our memories. And, as usually happens, we then start desiring it, as "early adopters" engage with the trend, we see it more and more (usually after we have gotten onto the train too) - and we start thinking, oh no, now even the uncool people wear my style, this style is no longer cool. The key may be intact, I still recognize the style and brand, but the desire that had before charged the key is now depleted and the feeling tone of the somatic marker has changed.

The perhaps most common scenario in popular imagination of this sensual "touch" is two people who cannot take their eyes off each other. As one seeks the attention of another, the attention is actually already "touching" the other, feeling around for signals (what attitude does the clothing reveal? what could be a commonality? is there a chance for a connection? etc). These signals tell something of how the scenario may develop - how people are oriented in action. As our attention is seeking signals and signs of what kind of person it is we are look at, we are already projecting scenarios and fantasies before even talking to the other. Only some of these imaginations are conscious, many are replayed from memory and social cues, what happened in other scenarios, movies, pretend plays or ideas of what our peers throughout our life have approved of as the right course of action. If there are glances back, the appearance has caught the observer. Through the way they now act, in the smallest gestures and glances, they could end up saying that he or she "cannot take his/her eyes off" the other. The attention was actively gripped by the other, and it may end up that in memory, the scene keeps replaying in their minds. The experience may even deprive them of sleep for weeks.

The situation above posits that clothes enact cognition both outwards (grabbing attention) as well as inward (activating memories, images, emotions). Neuroscientist Antonio Damasio posits how our sense of self, and thus our whole cognitive system, is "oriented" in certain directions; it is trained and tuned to certain sensibilities.[84] By being oriented, the self has prepared scenarios and attuned the perceptual apparatus towards a certain field of interest and emotional responses. If I am oriented towards football, I have interest in it, have studied the game, know the rules and have a "feeling" for the qualities of this interest. I know what signals and signs to look for that are crucial for understanding and appreciating the game; I know what to expect, and my attention follows suit.. In a similar vein, this is also how cultural theorist Sara Ahmed argues sexual "orientation" works on us: I have emotional responses prepared for certain cues in my cognition, and thus my whole self can become emotionally mobilized by such cues, involving memories, fantasies, projections of future action and pleasures.[85] Similarly, clothing orients us towards many bodily as well as cultural signals, all because of some cues my perception has touched in the clothing of someone else.

What we usually think of as "taste" is in material and embodied practice more like an orientation: an attunement of the sensorium and priming of mentalizations towards a certain environment and community. I may have a taste for a certain style of music or cuisine, but behavior wise, this means I have experience of engaging with that environment so I have managed to train my sensorium to appreciate its many varieties. For example, if I enjoy the music of 1980's British Heavy

Metal, I most probably have had friends also attuned to it and we have shared time and attention to emotionally mobilize our sensibilities to that form of music and scene. Similarly, if I have a taste for Italian cuisine, I have eaten it and enjoyed the company of friends with similar orientation of attention. It is the social and emotional feedbacks I have gotten along certain orientations that have produced my taste.[86]

But my prosthesis may also fail me and, in the same way that we only sense our skin at the extremes of our experiences, we become aware of our clothes in pain or pleasure. A stain can make a garment wounded - it can make the dress "fail" as aesthetic and embodied enhancement, and instead deflate the sense of self. Most of us have experienced such "wardrobe malfunction" at some point in our lives.[87] If we think back it may not have been so much a rational experience a much as an emotional one in which we lost self-esteem and a sense of sartorial worth. Indeed, the experience can feel much like a wound and we experience a social pain through the garment, our prosthetic limb. A heel may break, pants unbutton, or a dress rips: in most cases we can easily convince ourselves that we are still the same person, no part of fleshy body is hurt, yet we feel broken and incomplete. The garment now fails to enhance us, or touch others. It does not do what it is supposed to do. My cognitive sensorium shrinks, my posture contracts, and, like a snail, I only want to withdraw into my shell, but my shell is broken.

This is where the neural circuitry for physical and social pain overlap. A wardrobe malfunction hurts, even in the absence of any physical pain, yet such social pain is associated with somatic symptoms through shared activation in the brain. The pain from exclusion and shame is real.[88]

What the examples above show is how the embodied cognition mobilizes many parts of the self for possessing the social environment: we sense our clothing from the highly malleable social self-image, where I can change outfits to also change my orientations, all the way to the deeper "spine" of our emotions, the body-schema, the map of our internal milieu. If my outfit works, I may feel the attention of others, sense how they look at me, and I may feel it in my spine or it may arouse me, turning up the heat of my body or making me blush. Similarly, the wardrobe malfunction may feel like a blow to my body, my posture may take on a wounded stance and all I want to do is get out of my skin, change and become someone else. All the self is engaged in clothing. We must now unpack how the many layers of the self is formed and accentuated with the help of clothes.

....

A middle aged lawyer, working at a conservative office. Like
people of his trade, he is expected to wear suit and tie to work.
Each morning he diligently irons the shirt of the day while
listening to the morning news.

"As soon as I wake up I think of what shirt to wear."

He could leave the shirts to the dry cleaner, but there is
something in the ritual. It's a good start of the day.

"My daily challenge is to not wear the same combination of
suit, shirt and tie for at least a month."

He sees it as a mathematical problem to solve as much as an
aesthetic one. He has to think carefully of day's schedule in
advance, and choosing shirt is a way of preparing for what to
come.

"Most clients don't like surprises, so you have to be careful. It's
in the atmosphere of the room, you know."

He emphasises he is not an entertainer, "I represent people's
lives. I take no chances."

....

"On the train, I always take out my piercings. It's a bit like dressing down."

A goth in her mid 20s, dressed in dark and distressed street style. She talks about her visits to her grandmother at a nursing home on Long Island.

"Not that I am afraid of what my grandmother will think, or that I am prude. I think it is more a question of respect. I mean, I know that *she knows*. Mom was worried in the beginning so I know they spoke. It's more about the relationship I have with my grandmother. I like that special connection. I tell her everything. But somehow, it is as if the piercings get in the way. If I have them in, *she would see right through me.*"

．．．．．．．．．．．．．．．．．．．．．

At an airport in Sweden, you can immediately recognize
them. It is winter, yet they come into the arrival hall in
flip-flops, tanned and in tank tops, ikat or batik pants. Some
of the boys with thin beards. Just back from their Forbidden
Planet orbit; month long journeys in south-east Asia,
slavishly following the protocols of self-discovery. For the
coming weeks they struggle with their wardrobes. The
garments which were so right with their fellow backpackers
from Germany and Australia, at beaches and long journeys
on village roads, now feel awkwardly out of place. The first
few days they tell their old friends about their adventures,
but soon the old arrangements are back. Once again wearing
the same winter jackets they had before they left, the sense of
freedom they felt overseas dims with the falling snow. The
excitement fades together with the tan.

We have to ask what is it we risk as we gamble with fashion? A lawyer professes his lust for modest adventure in his combination of shirts and ties, yet doesn't want to risk his clients' fates. A young goth seems to desire to take off a mask when meeting her grandmother, while also confessing a fear of revealing what is underneath. The sense of selfhood a young traveler develops on a long journey retreats into idealized memory when back amongst old habits and friends.

As the people in the cases point out to us, the thing we call "self" is not so cohesive and unified as we may think, yet we still feel as one coherent person.[89] With some introspection we may uncover the many aspects of self we have or share, and how they have evolved. Nevertheless, our experience of the body is "tightly integrated within a bodily self-consciousness that offers a single but layered experience of one's body and oneself."[90] These layers, ranging from the physical, perceptual experience of my own body schema, to the self-image I perceive in the mirror, are integrated into my sense of self as much as the person perceived by others. Even if we experience our conception of self as coherent and authentic, we are in a dynamic process of continuous recreation. Indeed, it is a wonder how easily most people can adapt to new environments, attune ourselves to new acquaintances, learn new skills or recover from many types of injuries due to the plasticity of our neurons.

The boundary of our self seems intuitive: it is the skin. The skin is the membrane that acts as a boundary between self and the surrounding world. We often feel pain and have phobias around this boundary being pierced. A doctor's visit often concerns the breach of the membrane and we feel quiet discomfort at the procedures which invade our bodies, from the sight of blood, needles and syringes. It may thus be counterintuitive to think of the body as extending beyond the flesh and into the realm of clothing, even if we call it a "second skin." In my everyday experience, I may understand that there is a difference between my ordinary self and my dressed-up self, and I may experience a certain freedom as I dress "away" from my ordinary everyday role in society.[91]

A lawyer at a conservative office perhaps tests a patterned tie to challenge the boundaries and tastes of the office. But he knows what signals to look for if it is too much. He senses when his attention is being pulled to their gaze and away from his work. A backpacker dresses in ethnic clothes on the long overseas journey as part of some path of self discovery, while still not sticking out at the evening dinners at the hostel.

The masked and anonymous self is always slightly uncontrolled socially, not unlike how the feminine "mask" of make-up has culturally been regarded as a form of deception, or "made-up."[92] Wearing a mask is an experience which can make the masquerade joyful, but also the masked killer in horror movies so frightening, or the unease amongst the police as demonstrators wear balaclavas. Appearance is a mask, yet perhaps paradoxically, it brings us closer, as Oscar Wilde famously argues, "Give him a mask, and he will tell you the truth."

Even if my emotional life may change depending on context and company, the feeling I experience is still firmly anchored in my body. My mood, feelings, and emotions, correspond to my body states. We may quite easily recognize fear and pain on bodily responses, and also hunger or desire since we feel them as specific physical sensations throughout the body, such as a shiver in the spine, a "jump" of the heart, or as "butterflies" in the belly. But also more complex emotions run through my body, such as pride or shame. In many ways, my emotions are in my body, in the way that *I am my posture*. As Damasio suggests,

> "Can one imagine a more distinct body posture than that of the person beaming with pride? What exactly *beams*? The eyes to be sure, wide open, focused and intent on taking on the world; the chin held high; the neck and torso as vertical as they can get; the chest unfearingly filled with air; the steps firm and well planted. These are just some bodily changes we can *see*."[93]

Often, our emotions are also transmitted through garments. For example, the broken heel not only changes body posture, it changes the whole emotional scheme of the shamed and crippled wearer: it affects the sense of self. At its most extreme, such an experience may leave the wearer feeling as if the mindset does not matter: I "know" I shouldn't care, but my whole bodily experience is too overpowering. In that way we are like a paramecium, a simple unicellular organism. As Damasio suggests, such organism is "all body, no brain, no mind, swimming speedily away from a possible danger".[94] I may play with heels, yet I bet with emotions I feel in my whole body: the gamble is mobilizing my whole bodily emotion.[95]

American philosopher William James draws similar conclusions as he explores the self in his famous book *The Principles of Psychology*, where he touches upon how clothes plays an important, yet often neglected, part in the creation of the self.[96] James differs between what he calls the material self, the social self, the spiritual self and the pure Ego. If our body is at the core of the material self, the clothes also come to define this self, as "the clothes comes next [...] The old saying that the human person is composed of three parts - soul, body, and clothes - is more than a joke."[97] And James continues,

> "We so appropriate our clothes and identify ourselves with them that there are few of us who, if asked to choose between having a beautiful body clad in raiment perpetually shabby and unclean, and having an ugly and blemished form always spotlessly attired, would not hesitate a moment before making a decisive reply."[98]

It may come as no surprise that most of us care about clothes, not only for social pressures, but for the way they make us *feel* the world around us and *places* the self emotionally in the world. We may claim we don't care, but when someone exclaims "I would *never* wear that," it is often with a such conviction in their voice, we can hear the emotional grounding of that claim: this body would cringe with shame in such an outfit.

So how could we understand the self in order to see how the gamble of fashion can be anchored into our emotional life? There are many ways to frame the self, and psychology has a long history of typologies such as body/soul, conscious/unconscious, id/ego etc. To pinpoint the embodied perspective of fashion, we have chosen a model in correspondence with Damasio's work on emotions.[99] We want to highlight a continuum of the self which interacts with fashion, from the person we feel we are, and say we are, and all the way to that uncanny feeling that the more I am myself, the more I am somehow imitating others. We must first start with the production of the self.

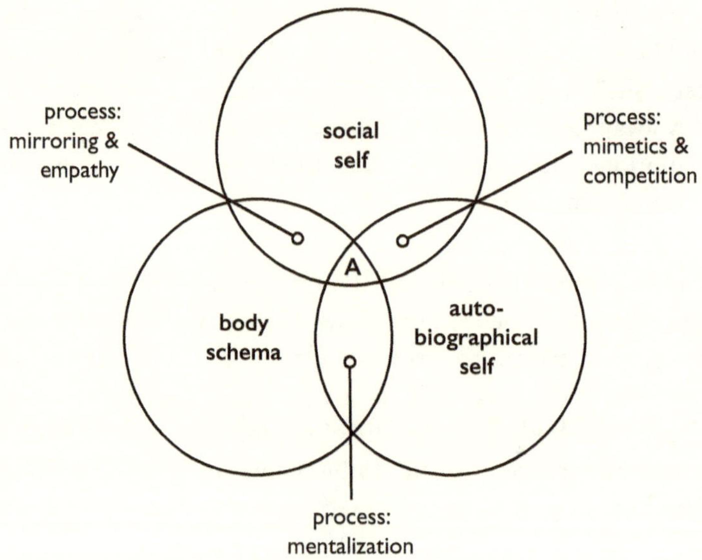

Three environments of self.
(A) Ideal self & Fashion Phantom

We can say the self develops in conjunction with our ability to sense various environments. The resulting selves are three environments: a *body-schema*, an *auto-biographical self* and a *social self*. The *body schema* is our interoception, exteroception and proprioception, the neural "maps" we have of our own body in our mind and the resulting ability to sense our body acting or being in the world. This sense of self is formed from the interaction with our physical environment. The *auto-biographical self* is the reflective inner world built on the memory of past actions, their intentionality and feedback, but also imagined environments and scenarios, which we use to test and enhance our agency in the world. The *social self* is formed from our interactions with others. It is the persona, the roles we play in society, and how we act in relation to others.

Between these environments there are three main processes; the process of *mentalization*, self-reflection and self awareness through abstract thinking and scenario-building, the process of *empathy*, knowing the emotions of others through the body, without conscious awareness, and the processes of *mimetics and competition*, through which we gain social roles in the games and hierarchies of social life. All these processes and environments play part in the constructing the (clothed) ideal self-image - what we call the "fashion phantom" - which plays the main part in animating fashion from being an object in the external world and to become an inherent part of our emotional life and self-image.[100]

Author and semiotician Umberto Eco also explores the body's relation to clothing in a story which may lead us into the embodied experience of fashion. In this story, "Lumbar thought," Eco describes how the jeans become popular in the 1970s and he buys a pair.[101] He is surprised of their fit, how they squeeze his body, and this changes his attention and thinking (this is long before stretch denim). The jeans cling onto the body in a specific way, that is, "the sensation of wearing pants that, instead of clutching the waist, held the hips, because it is a characteristic of jeans to grip the lumbar-sacral region and stay up thanks not to suspension but to adherence." The jeans don't pinch, but they "made their presence felt," as Eco notices, and he senses "a kind of sheath around the lower half of my body." To put Eco's observation in the context of our study, he senses the jeans and his newly felt body through the fit and the constitution of the stiff denim fabric, affecting the motion of the hips. Connecting back to cognition, his perception of both the body and the world has changed. He senses his body differently through his proprioceptive systems, through the snug fit and constitution of the stiff, denim fabric. His embodied cognition has changed. As Eco notices, the garment starts to affect his body and posture, "I discovered that my movements, my way of walking, turning, sitting, hurrying, were different. Not more difficult, or less difficult, but certainly different." In the stiff garment, Eco's body-schema is been modified, his posture is different and his body moves as if in an armor.

But the jeans also changes Eco's self-awareness and auto-biographical self. His body tells him another story of the encounter with the world and through mentalization, it modifies his intentions and agency. As Eco continues, "I lived in the knowledge that I had jeans on, whereas normally we live forgetting that we're wearing undershorts or trousers. I lived for my jeans, and as a result I assumed the exterior behavior of one who wears jeans. In any case, I assumed a demeanor." From a neurological perspective, what Eco put his finger on is how the sensation of the garment has affected his body-schema, but also his affects, attention and thinking. This leads Eco to see himself as a different agent in the world; his self-image has been modified, he does not only live "in" his jeans, but he lives "for" them.

Eco goes on to discuss how this type of transformative clothing has played a central role in the social construction of self. For example, women's "experiences of this kind are familiar because all their garments are conceived to impose a demeanor—high heels, girdles, brassieres, pantyhose, tight sweaters."

> "I thought then about how much, in the history of civilization, dress as armor has influenced behavior and, in consequence, exterior morality. The Victorian bourgeois was stiff and formal because of stiff collars; the nineteenth-century gentleman was constrained by his tight redingotes, boots, and top hats that didn't allow brusque movements of the head."[102]

In every age, bodies are imprisoned into sartorial packages that give shape to their behavior, but they are not necessarily imposed from above by dictate, no, we often *desire them*. We mirror ourselves in others, that is how we grow empathy and cultivate our sense of self through cultural imitation and behaviors, and clothes are part of our performance.[103] But we also mimic our idols and use this imitation as leverage in competitions with peers. Through such social processes we come to use clothing and fashion as amplifications and expressions of our aspirations and desires; I get a new pair of sneakers so I can run faster to compete with my older brother, or I buy a similar pair of pants as my idol to test out a new social scene and tell an updated story about myself to my peers. These garments create a new sense of self in relation to my peers, and I project this in relation to my ideal sense of self, how I imagine myself being at my best. This imaginary self is anchored deeply in my body and the processes of self-awareness, and I continually use it to not only see and judge myself, but to sense and compare myself to others. This ideal self is my own "fashion phantom." Indeed, with the gamble of fashion, my sense of self changes as it is set to play, from the deep body-schema of proprioception to the socialized ideal self: the ideal self is put to test.

The three selves

The three selves are entangled in a continuous dynamic and we will try to unpack them so we can more in detail understand the gambling processes which produce our fashioned self-image, or what we call the fashion phantom.

As mentioned shortly before, our body as a living organism is in constant change. The process keeping the body alive is more dynamic than static, so "homeodynamics" may be a more appropriate term for a flexible process of environmental adjustment, rather than the more consistent and conservationist "homeostasis."[104] Similarly, while the experience of self may feel like a coherent and unitary experience, neuro-imaging and neurological data suggest that the self includes several experiential layers that are constantly re-formed through our interaction with our internal and external worlds, involving dimensions of space, time, as well as the influences of other people.[105] To put it plainly, each self is a representation of our place in a certain environment, and each self changes as we develop our capacity to sense different dimensions of our environments (from the body, memories and to the social self). We modify these selves by creating neural maps of our environment and patterns of interaction, called image schemas. These selves are largely unconscious to us, and are revealed when things go wrong or through experimentation, where we push our boundaries. The layers of self are created through trial-and-error, through gamble and play.

Body Schema

We will begin with the basis of self, known as body schema. Our body schema is a primordial sense of embodied self-unity, providing the capacity to separate our own embodied existence from the outside world: I am present in my body.[106] A non-conscious state that is our moment-to-moment consciousness of self.[107] It is produced by a collection of neural patterns conducted by a system of neurons in the brainstem and spinal cord that extend nerve endings to respiratory and digestive mucous membranes, gathering information such as our heart rate and bowel movements. In addition to detecting information required for essential processes (breathing, heart rate, digestion, and temperature). The system's regular, automatic sensing of the internal body state allows it to detect the physical changes which affect the homeostasis (or homeodynamics) of the organism,[108] making it the basis of the ability of the body to distinguish from good or bad, positive or negative, pleasure or pain, attraction or repulsion. The activity of this system, in addition to being responsible for consciousness, is also the basis of emotion.[109]

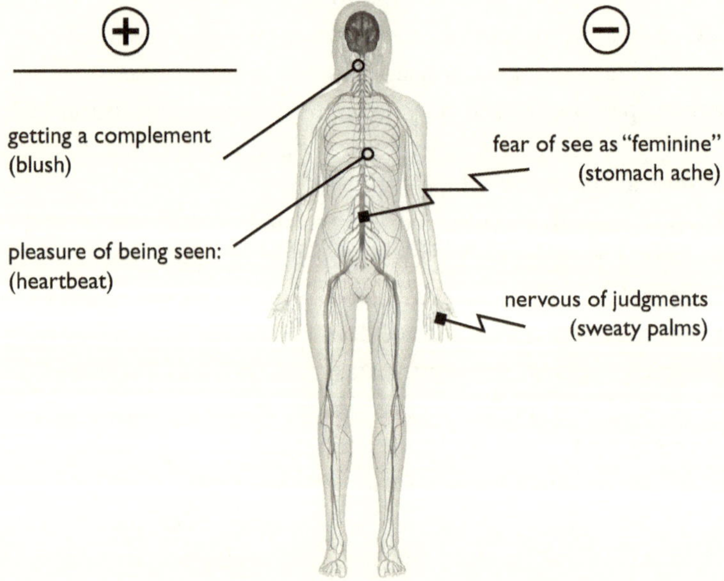

Body schema - somatic markers (approximations)

Next, in early childhood, we develop the ability to sense our external spatiotemporal environments through perception and action, resulting in a more complex body representation.[110] Through the rapid development of recently evolved areas of the brain, we develop the ability to perceive the sounds, smells, images, and textures of our environment,[111] and map them onto our brains to create an internal representation of our external environments. These senses, when combined, result in the ability to perceive where our bodies are and how they move in relation to this environment, called proprioception. This sixth sense informs us of the position of our bodies in space, the relative position of neighboring parts of the body, and the speed and directions of our movements. Similar to our perception of internal environments, we translate this information into neural maps, images translating the active landscapes of our emotions active across our bodies.[112]

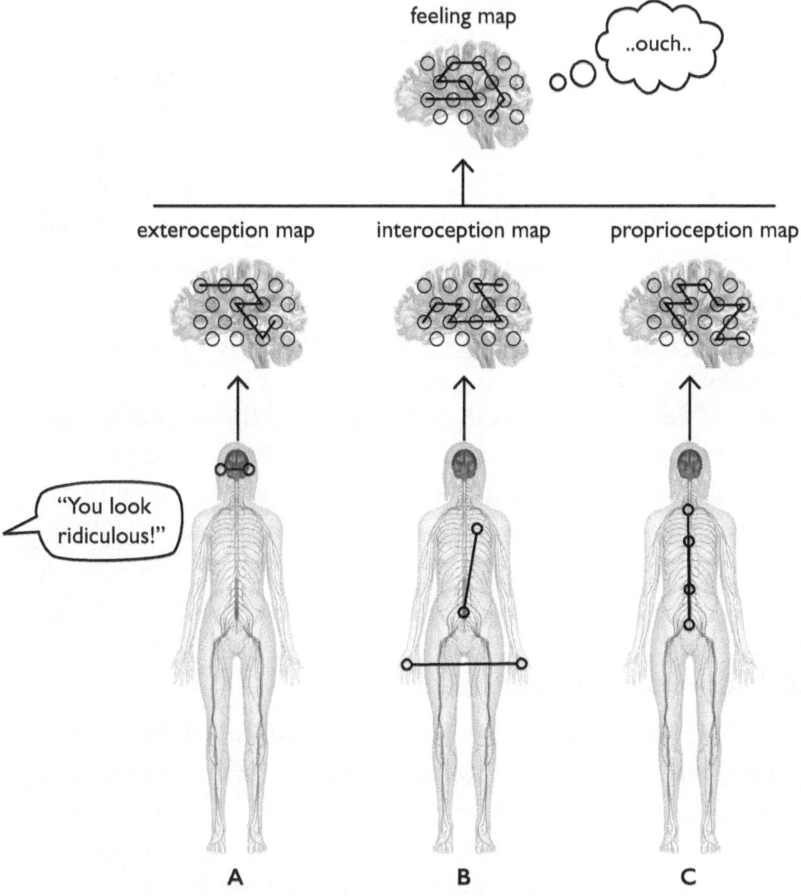

Image-schemas;
neural maps combining different somatic markers for shame (A) sense of being watched, (B) sweaty palms, racing heart and uneasy stomach, (C) spine bends, posture shrinks

Complex emotions emerge through combinations of somatic markers. As Damasio posits,

> "I ask the reader to imagine a state of pleasure (or anguish) and try to itemize its components by making a brief inventory of the varied part so the body that are changed in the process: endocrine, cardiac, circulatory, respiratory, intestinal, epidermic, muscular. Now consider the feeling you will experience is the integrate perception of all such changes as they occur in the landscape of the body." [113]

While we might often experience crises of our social and emotional identities and status, our physical self seems to be relatively stable and unchanging. You never go to bed worrying that you will wake up having incorporated an object as part of your body, or will feel strongly that your arm is no longer yours to own: the body schema tends to stay the same. But experiments and disorders crack this facade of stability. Instead if being fixed, our body schemas are constantly updated and actively formed through a dynamic process of perception and integration that occurs without our conscious knowledge. [114]

As exemplified in Eco's story before, clothes also make up our tactile and visual environment and our interactions with clothing have a significant bearing on our body schema. From the minute we are born we are wrapped in the environment of the textures and pressure of textiles on our skin. It is the immediate interaction that our skin has of the world. For example, wearing new shoes may at first feel restrictive, but we quickly adapt our gait, just like Eco does to his new pants.

Auto-biographical (personal) self

Through continued interaction with the world and the development of areas in the brain that allow us to map and organize our internal and external experiences across longer periods of time, we form personal memories of our past; memories characterized by temporal, spatial, and self-referential features. [115] Yet these rudimentary episodes often contain risk: the experience of jumping over an obstacle, or learning the outcome of a gymnastic trick. The auto-biographical self focuses on the stories you gain from learned experiences. Yet, as all experiences are emotionally tainted, the autobiography of the self becomes based on emotional memories. If I fail to jump over the obstacle without witnesses, my jumping may be restricted primarily by inability, but if it happens before others, my inability may come from shame. Indeed, any sense of movement with my body may be tainted by estrangement and fearfulness. These episodic memories are tied to our capacity to understand ourselves in terms of subjective states and imagine future states. Our memory allows us to form a dynamic, internal narrative with a lived past and an anticipated future: what Damasio calls an auto-biographical self.[116]

Like the body schema, memories are fluid and dynamic, created and re-created over time. The mood and context in which we retell memories affect their emotional coloring. Self-awareness emerges as the self comes to mind, aware of itself over time as a sensing and emotional point of reference. As Damasio suggests, "conscious minds begin when self comes to mind, when brains add a self process to the mind mix, modestly at first but quite robustly later."[117] We also start to learn and develop the networks in our brains that are responsible for carrying out the types of internally-oriented, cognitive processes that happen during rest. For example, we begin to make sense of ourselves and each other in terms of subjective states (i.e. beliefs, desires, hopes, fears) and mental processes through mentalization; imagining various scenarios and responses.[118] We process memories and produce imaginary plans and thus gain the ability to test out possible future scenarios through imagination, imagining and telling new stories of our lives.[119]

Cognitive psychologist Alison Gopnik has written extensively about children's use of imitation and imagination to learn about the causal structure of the world. What Gopnik has found is how pretend play builds a playful persona in our head that we use to test possibilities and probabilities, causation and correlation.[120] With imagination we explore hypothesis and train behavior without actually doing it in the physical world, and as Gopnik has shown, we need this imaginary training in order to understand the minds of others. Not only does this concern others, but our imagination needs to be trained in order to make our imaginary inventions more accurate. For example, an inventor, engineer or craftsman will have a very accurate way of building mental models, "seeing" how they connect and are built in his or her "inner vision" while an amateur's image is usually very fuzzy on the edges.[121]

The process of dressing requires memories of previous experiences and selves. From gestures, knowing how to best get a sweater over the head, to affective recollections on how to match it with other garments in the process of remembering emotionally grounded experiences. This forms a special dressed sense of self, as well as helping to imagine future scenarios. Fashion scholar Joanne Entwistle puts the spotlight on this practice of dressing as she argues,

> "The individual and very personal act of getting dressed is an act of preparing the body the social world, making it appropriate, acceptable, indeed respectable and possibly even desireable also. Getting dressed is an ongoing practice, requiring knowledge, techniques and skills, from learning how to tie our shoelaces and do up our buttons as children, to understanding about colours, textures and fabrics and how to weave them together to suit our bodies and our lives. Dress is the way in which individuals learn to live in their bodies and feel at home in them."[122]

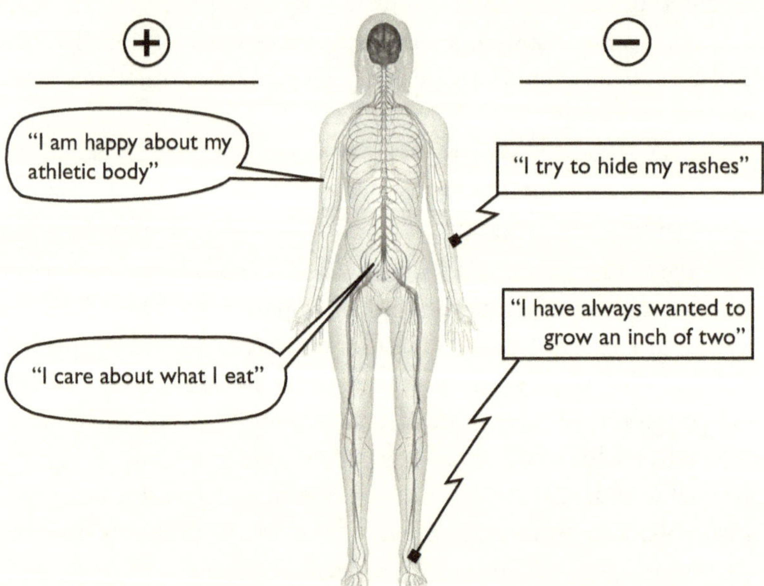

Auto-biographical self (approximations)

It is the memories of past interactions of dress that makes us "feel home in" these garments. As we engage in dressing, we *feel* out what works and what does not work, and in the process we form a mental memory of self: we tell and *feel* a non-verbal story of who we are and who we present ourselves to be. We play with these stories and test out new combinations, challenging boundaries, what "works" and what is "too much." It is not so much an articulation as much as an emotional coordination with peers and the people we seek everyday affirmation from, between the values we share; music, lifestyle, culture, class, community: where we feel emotionally "at home." But we also tell who we strive to be, where we want to go, what stories we seek to tell. Through mentalization, we can be aware of how we feel or think in a certain situation and, over time, become better at projecting and making predictions about how we might feel in similar situations in the future. These processes allow us to recognize how we are feeling in an outfit right now and help us plan our dress before an important date or job interview, perhaps laying sleepless the night before.

We use similar types of practical imagination in the dressing room - what fits with what clothes - are these pants the right length for the boots I love to show off? Thus, in a similar vein to the engineer or craftsman, we can imagine the overall silhouette of a nice outfit. Yet it will require aesthetic imagination and accurate visioning to make the pieces, patterns and colours match together when it comes to the case of *actually wearing* the outfit (and how that raises emotions in the body). Often we *think* some pieces of dress may look nice together, but we fail to mentalize accurately their precise combination, and the look disappoints us in the real world: it doesn't *feel right.*

Aesthetic mentalization processes require active training and continuous updating, and as our wardrobes and body shapes change, the process is developed and we grow a sense of what we call "personal taste." That is, a historical assemblage of outfits that have "worked" for us and that we keep coming back to.[123] Indeed, the very notion of "having character" may both connote someone brave to dress in a bold manner (consistently over time and perhaps with a special quirkiness), but it may also signify an anxious trait where my auto-biographical self has become petrified which makes the person uncomfortable to fully engage with a living and changing world.[124]

Social Self

Mentalization is also a profoundly social construct, allowing people to think about and feel the mental states of others. With some empathy, you can feel what someone feels in a moment of joy or sadness. Similarly, the emotional rush could be experienced as you see the new confidence your friend radiates in a new jacket. As you learn more from real experiences and play, you become better at imagining possible future mental states, and also the modulations of desires they evoke. One learns to play the game, bet on desires and raise the stakes.[125]

While mentalizing is often considered a conscious process, it has recently been shown to play out at the subconscious level through the discovery of "mirror neurons." Mirror neurons make us experience the actions and emotions you see in others on an unconscious level.[126] In humans, these neurons have also been found in areas of the brain tied to emotion, which means that when you observe the actions and feelings of others, these neurons become active and unconsciously recreate the chemical processes that would happen in your body if you were to act or feel the same way as the first person. In other words, mirror neurons provide a neural basis of "empathy and comprehension, transmission, contagion, and sharing of feelings, emotions and mood."[127]

This capacity to perform internally-oriented mental processes and mentalizing about others provides a neural basis for the development of a socially embedded self-concept; how we shape our sense of self by internalizing our perception of other people's mental states. We use this ability to think about ourselves and others in terms of minds and mental states to create complex social arrangements and navigate our interpersonal worlds.

This means that as you watch someone seem happy about the attention she gets because of her clothing, mirror neurons replicate these emotions in your own brain and body. If the emotion is strong enough, you will form an emotional memory of this unconscious experience and use it to guide your actions in the future without your awareness. Unknowingly, your desires and intentions have been affected. And even if you may have a clue, we seldom admit to ourselves how we imitate or look up to others. If I acknowledge I look up to others, it undermines my self-esteem: "am I not good enough?" Indeed, admitting to the emotion of envy is a form of social double-bind: I admit I care what others do, while simultaneously recognizing to myself that they are superior to me as I look up to them, heightening my feeling of inferiority.[128]

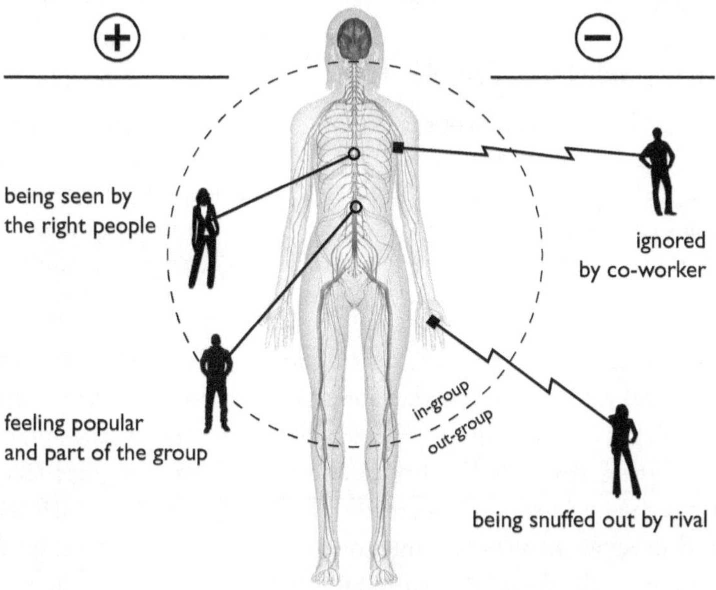

Social self (approximations)

To think of ourselves as unified and autonomous, we put labels on our traits, ordering them according to social conceptions and norms. On this basic level, the social self is the role we present of ourselves in the world, my gender, profession or title. As Erving Goffman has famously shown, we have several selves that we present on different "stages" in our world, not unlike theatre: the person we are at home or when visiting the grandparents may be different from the one we present at work or at the nightclub.[129] They share the same physical body and memories, but the different social selves trigger various body schema and auto-biographical selves, making us live in different affectual spheres which in turn enact different behaviors and desires.[130]

In the social world we cultivate an "objectified body", a public representation of our own body, mapped as knowledge in our mind.[131]

This social self is a knowledge of the body parts and actions of others, an objectified public representation of our own body: the body that others see, and more importantly, that they can judge and evaluate.[132] As already noted by Freud's conflict between Id, Ego, and Superego, the development of the objectified body is emotionally troubling for the individual, who often encounters inconsistent feedback from the social world, as well as from the individual emotional grounding.[133] As suggested by psychologist Paul Schilder,

> "…the child takes parts of the bodies of others into its own body-image. It also adopts in its own personality the attitude taken by others towards parts of their own bodies. [...] There exists a deep community between one's own body-image and the body-image of others. In the construction of the body-image there is a continual testing to discover what could be incorporated in the body"[134]

The objectified self is the marker in gamble of the self: what marks position and value, what we place on the social board to represent our aspirations. It is a socially imprinted self and is thus a relational construct, cutting through the body-schema and autobiographical self. Whereas the body-schema is created through interaction with the inner and outer environment, and thus exists in relation to how these environments change, the auto-biographical self is created in relation to experiences and time. The social self is created through relations and interactions with the social environment, through play, comparison and social games.[135] The social self cannot emerge in isolation, but we need to train relationships through some basic form of social life, and these interactions come to define our self-image.[136]

Our social self is also touching the world through its senses, such as the social senses of relationship, closeness and trust.[137] As neuroscientist Paul MacLean argues, "A sense of separation is a condition that makes being a mammal so painful."[138] And separation is something felt in the body, it is mapped onto our limbic system, in the neural maps of interoception. Therefore, when we say that someone "broke my heart" or "hurt my feelings" these are not merely metaphors, but speak of neurological sensibilities.[139] Such affects confirm how our brains evolved to "experience threats to our social connections in much the same way they experience physical pain," activating the same neural circuitry as that of physical pain, for example to ensure the survival of our children by helping them stay close to parents.[140] It is this sociability of the brain that makes fashion such an emotionally laden skin. The judgment of fashion brings us closer to others, or separates us, and these emotions are tied to our limbic system.[141]

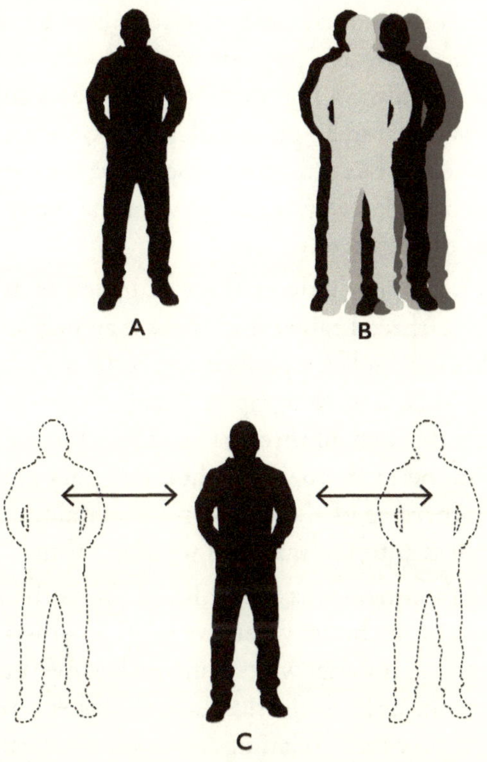

Conceptions of self in context;
(A) individual, (B) dividual, (C) inter-dividual

A fruitful way to think of the social self is to use French neuropsychiatrist Jean-Michel Oughourlian's idea of psychology being not so much about the individual as much as the "interdividual." This term puts the finger on how we are always divided through the relationships with our peers, but it is still more than a "dividual," a self-hood tied to and aligned with peers through mutual relationships. Both the concepts of the "dividual" and the "inter-dividual" stress we are not "ourselves" as much as we would like to think: my experience of "self" is always a *social self*.[142] Instead of existing in isolation, the social self is always formed in recurrent relationships with peers, friends and enemies (not only Mother and Father). Oughourlian posits, the monadic subject doesn't exist, that the self is formed only in relations with the other, and that psychology cannot focus on individuals but only on rapports and relationships.[143] With the inter-dividual, Oughourlian stresses that the dividual is caught up in tensions of the in-between, in conflicts and rivalries. As Oughourlian has it, we are "puppets of desire," and our desires are not only our own, but always imitated from our peers and the people whose judgment we care for. To put it differently, we are not in-dividual or autonomous selves, but our sense of self always exists in-between and in relation to others, always torn between the many parts of our own self as well as the selves of others.

Oughourlian differs between three main processes of the mind, or what he calls the "three brains," and these may help us unpack the constitution of the social self. Oughourlian's model of "brains" overlaps with the body-schema, auto-biographical self and social self, as the three processes cut through all three parts of self. But we will here focus on the third, "mimetic" brain, as Oughourlian puts a strong emphasis on the social processes of the brain and the importance of seeing how we are much less autonomous than we might think.[144]

What Oughourlian calls the "third brain" is the mimetic and relational processes of the brain, where we relate to others in ways that are first and foremost mimetic: we continuously copy others and imitate behaviours we like or find effective. Like the other selves, the social self is a continuous process of relations, constantly recreating itself, remapping emotional valence onto the body-schema and auto-biographical self. As Damasio suggests, the self is "a perpetually re-created neurobiological state,"[145]

> "At each moment the state of self is constructed, from the ground up. It is an evanescent reference state, so continuously and consistently reconstructed that the owner never knows it is being remade unless something goes wrong with the remaking."[146]

To Oughourlian, this third brain is where we relate to the world "personally" (as in the production of self), in continuous relation to, and mimicking of, our peers. "The third brain, the mimetic brain, is the one that introduces the little human to sociability, to relations with others, to the interdividual rapport, and indeed to humanness."[147] It is the third brain that puts us "in tune" to our peers, synchronizing mimetics and emotions and which handles the paradoxical formation of self, where we feel we are unique yet still are on the same "wavelength" as our friends, imitating their tastes, stimulations and behavior, so we end up listening to the same music, enjoy going to same places, and share time and experiences, and dressing alike. We may experience we live in the first two brains, in thinking and feeling, but as Oughourlian has it, "the first and second brains are, so to speak, pulled along by the third brain."[148] Our cognitive apparatus as well as our thinking and feeling, are bound into mimetic relations, imitating others and learning to de-sire the same desires as our peers, but deep in the brain,

> "the mimetic relation, reverberates its effects on the cortical and limbic brains: it will go into the wardrobe of the first brain in order to coif itself in economic, political, moral, or religious justifications and rationaliza-tions, and in the wardrobe of the second brain to dress in the matching emotions, feelings, and moods."[149]

Our sense of self is thus highly contradictory, continually recreating itself in the interaction between the three brains, and purposefully "for-getting" how influenced we are by others. Also because the act of copy-ing produces internal conflict as well as social antagonism.[150] The use of fashion in the process of creating a sense of self circulates through the three brains, from the unconscious imitation of others, to the emo-tional charge of certain looks, to the rationalization processes where we make up reasons for why we dress in certain ways, and then back around again.

Thus we are much more affected by fashion than we like to admit: it is amalgamated with a part of our brain's architecture to mimic our peers.[151] It is this third mimetic brain that deals with syn-chronizing these conflicting functions of the formation of self, as it always contains the tensions between self and others. As Rene Girard has declared; "Imitative desire is always the desire to be Another."[152] Desires also have a very specific life in the formation of self, as Oughourlian also highlights, "desire fails when it succeeds: it disap-pears as soon as it possesses the object that it coveted."[153] The object has not changed physically, but its metaphysical status in my mind has changed.[154]

The fashioned self is always social, mimetic and relational, and always caught up in rivalries of desire. As fashion is per definition social, it compares itself to its mirror image and its desire is always set in relation to the desire of others. As I stand ambivalent in the morning, testing if I should tuck the shirt or not, or cuff the pants or not, I may only see myself in the mirror, yet in my body there are echoes of past experiences as well as images of my peers flashing through my emotions if a particular look "feels right" or not.

For example, I feel good in my new shoes, and I see myself in my inner self-image with my shoes on, and as I walk in the street I cannot help myself but cast a quick look to the shop windows to see my own reflection, "yeah, those shoes look good," affirming my inner image of self. My gait is longer, prouder, and my emotions ride high. In my thinking, I may suggest reasons for this to my rational brain, while at the same time unconsciously deny that I got these shoes in the first place because I saw someone I look up to wear them, and I knew these kicks would impress my peers. As the day passes, me and my shoes are on a perfect ego-trip together.

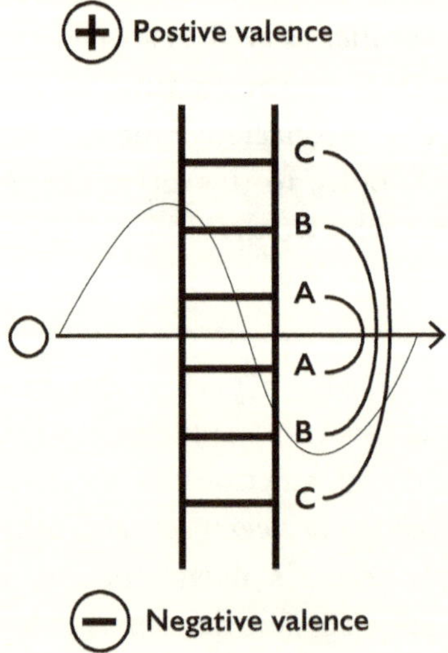

Ladder of failed desires
(A) Low risk, loss of interest, (B) identity investement,
influence rivalry, (C) high risk, absolute failure, leading to
loss of face, shame.

But if things go wrong, we could place these emotions on a "ladder of failed desires," ranging from simple disinterest to explicit rejection, or from careless ambigity to a social pain which make me lose the emotional rush from my much desired shoes. On the lowest rung we experience a loss of interest from the simple life of use, where the shoes lose the intensity of interest as my attention drifts elsewhere. A step higher may be that the shoes become "uncool" as other things overturn my fascination with the brand; a new style, a new competitive desire has upended the prime position of the shoes. On a higher rung, a rivalry kicks in as I see my social competitor wear the same shoes. "Outrageous! I saw them first!"

Suddenly the self-image is cracked, the emotional charge of the merged self-and-shoe image is damaged, even though nothing has actually happened between me and my shoes. In my own reasoning, I may invent excuses for my emotions and address them against my rival: "that person is not a real sneakerhead," she is always a copy-cat, she has no sense of style, etc, but the thrill is gone. On the highest step we can imagine the horror of misreading my own feeling of where the shoes work and they may be a cause of explicit rejection and bullying. My aesthetic aspirations are exposed and viciously attacked by enemies who use my own "armor" against me. After such attack my gait is no longer so stridently proud. My shoes "betrayed" me, and this side of my emotional self I may never dare to expose again.

In its milder form, we may all have experienced some form of sartorial rejection; "who do you think you are, wearing those shoes?" - which is another way of saying "you cannot sit with us!" The shoes, which I acquired as an entry ticket to the cool gang, not only did not work as a bridge into their community, but it was explicitly read as an unaccepted signal of my submission to the cool group's taste. I had tried to become one of them, to gain entry, and the entry was publicly refused. I was wearing my social ambition "on my sleeve" but my attempt was exposed and ridiculed. I am left humiliated and even my former peers now resent me for trying to advance socially, thus tacitly exposing that their company is not good enough for me.

Such everyday fashion stories may at first seem banal, and a recurrent trope in day-channel series, but they contain a central experience that most of us recognize: the proud merger we sometimes feel with some of our best garments, and sometimes, as they lose their magic, they may deeply affect our emotional balance. We may even turn to express something like magic exorcism: angry throwing the shoes in the hallway when coming home, or ritualistically sacrificing them to the trash, refusing to see them again. My sense of self has been hurt, my ideal me taken a hit, my self-esteem has been robbed by reality.

But it asks the question: "who" in me is it that actually got hurt? And how does this sense of self connect to the larger world of images, celebrities, prostheses and commodities?

A group of students in their late teens walk into the store after class. Their voices reverberate throughout the space as they move together, confidently.

They are on-trend with the 90's look, gravitating to the vinyl bubblegum mini dress with spaghetti straps and the straight neckline and some sleek black satin dresses. Eventually they move on to the cheetah patterned fur jacket with oversized shoulders, a long sequin dress from the 80s, with prominent shoulders.

"Grace that is *SO YOU*, I hope you're getting that."

"That looks amazing on you."
"Where am I going to wear it though?"

They leave with only a black tank-top. The other items stay on the racks for a more adventurous spirit.

....

A young woman is knocking on the door to her friend's place, wearing her Margiela Tabi shoes. She wears them all the time.

"I think they look really artsy."

Her friend's dad opens the door and calls down her daughter. While they wait, he eyes her shoes.

"You look like a horse." The leer in his voice makes the joke not sound funny at all.

She doesn't know what to say.

"You would look much better if you dressed like a lady..."

Back in the 2000s, when Uggs were really trendy, she would do anything to own a pair. Something about the light-brown color, the blocky shape, the white sheepskin just popping out over the top that could make her blend right in.

She knew her family couldn't afford them. They were the type to get everything on sale, and she'd never seen a discounted pair. One day her father called from abroad and asks her size over the phone. He had bought her a pair.

"I could not believe it, my heart literally jumped with joy."

When she wears them to school the first day, one of the girls (who had two pairs) claims loudly they are fake.

"I started arguing with her really angrily."

The girl walks away.

"But it was as if the boots had been spoiled. I didn't want to tell my parents."

The social reality of fashion is infused with wishful thinking and make-believe, or in the realm of looks, make-up. It is an enhanced and idealized form of appearances; it is about what *things appear to be, how things can be* and *how we wish them to be*. Fashion is the the feelings we have as we manifest a negotiated social imagination into an embodied and inter-dividually experienced reality.

The examples above expose some struggles between ideal selves and the inner integration of the objectified body (observed the unity of one's own body as through the eyes of others).[155] A pack of teens go out hunting for bargains, testing each other for who dares to pull off the cheetah look, yet none of them is courageous enough. A young woman, confident in her tabi shoes, has her ideal awkwardly snubbed by her friend's father. The authenticity of a pair of precious Ugg boots becomes a serious matter for someone striving to see herself as accepted by the cool girls.

Such stories may seem trivial, yet they highlight how the ideal self clashes with aspirations towards an ideal societal body, yet it is a quotidian experience and a normal social process. Its main outcome is a new representation—or "self-image"—that integrates the objectified representation of the personal body with the ideal societal body, the *ideal me*; ideals of behavior, appearances, performance and emotions.[156] As we have mentioned before, our social self is configured by peer-feedback, in a positive and negative direction, through pleasure and pain, attraction and rejection.[157] Yet the direction is not random, it is guided by societal ideals, or more specifically: by the ideals shared amongst our peers. By reflecting and leveraging these ideals to our advantage we seek affirmation and affection and get a sense of self-expansion.[158] These feedback cycles of agreement/disagreement relate to the pain/pleasure index and maps onto sensory experiences over time, creating somatic markers manifested in unconsciously held emotions and behaviors. Over time, images of perfection and patterns of tastes get mapped onto our cognitive models: we compare and judge, not only others but also ourselves. This means ideals are not something abstract, but something we learn to sense in our bodies. As Damasio suggests, such unconscious markers allow us to make efficient decisions when we are confused and stressed, when we are too tired to engage our consciousness, and thus much of our emotional life is playing out on unconscious levels of the mind. Sometimes the emotions surface and rise to our consciousness in feelings we can trace, but it is not always so.

Whereas Freud's super-ego was primarily repressive, the ideal self can be shaped perfectly in tune with hedonistic consumerism.[159] Equally me-centered and happily narcissistic, it idealizes its own elitist adoration, continuously reinforced by cultural memes: "Be what you can be," "Just do it," "Because I'm worth it!"[160] As sociologist Zygmunt Bauman argues, the marketplace is the main arena today for a formation of the self, where consumers are "simultaneously, *promoters of commodities* and the *commodities they promote.*"[161] Indeed, we today live in a society where we continuously need to compete, perform and achieve, and, after investing our time and soul in the projects of the self, if we are not one of those who is "making it" we are doomed as losers - or we have failed to live up to our own ideal.[162]

Yet most of us think we choose our clothes under some form of consistent aesthetic rationality, such as "my style is X or Y." This sense of having an "own style" is built on the assumption that we are fully conscious about how and why we dress in certain ways. Indeed, at some occasions we agonize and think perhaps too much of how we dress, such as the sartorial stress in the dredging process of choosing a wedding dress, or endless discussions on dress etiquette and cultural conventions which all seem far from unconscious, or similarly, the conscious choice *not* to seem to care, which is often an elaborate style in itself. But so much of our dress is emotional and hits upon somatic markers - producing the desired emotions through our bodies - and these define the person we project ourselves to be.

This inner projection of a desired self-appearance is the *ideal self*, or the dressed model me.[163] This ideal me is a construct, a tool, that gives direction to the continuous reconstruction of the full self, binding together the body-schema, auto-biographical self and social self, and compares it to the social norms, peers and competitors in the social as well as ideal realm. We watch and grow in relation to our peers as well as by idols, models, and archetypes. This ideal me is in itself a neural symbol or map, a clothed phantom that exists within us and helps guide us through uncharted social territory: a prosthetic of our imagination. It is an ideal that is always engaged in a gamble with the social reality of peer pressures, rivalries, hierarchies and desires, and it is a discord that ripples through the three layers of self.[164]

The ideal is at the center of the three selves, a slightly elevated, semi-reality that exists as a grasp-able embodiment of our desires.[165] As we have pointed out earlier, we call this self-image the "fashion phantom" as we claim it is a dressed figure: highly real in the neurological sense as a schema associated with somatic markers across the body, yet it also has ghost-like qualities; obtuse and imaginary, always slipping away. It is mirrored in sources outside ourselves, in peers and the world of mediated phantasma, at the same time both a social imagination and physical reality, and this image connects all layer into one coherent living experience. Fashion is both a social imagination, *phantasma*, a myth we live in, but the myth is manifested into our emotional experiences, it has real consequences and shapes our cognition and sense of self.[166] Like in the earlier story, the successful or failed shoes tell us something about the connection we make between our dressed body, our sense of self and our emotional life: these phenomena merge into a special image we have of our dressed self.

The fashion phantom

As is witnessed by the stories above, fashion lives in the current realm of our shared social imagination: it is a group struggle over who dares to wear what, but also about the authenticity of our aspirations (for example reflected in a pair of Ugg boots in the story above).[167] The people in the cases seem confident that they seek an evolvement and emergence of a new self by playing with their clothes. As we see this evolution, the people above seek a development of their *fashion phantom*, their embodied social self-image standing in relation to their ideal.

What we call the fashion phantom in our body is a ghost that ties us to the imaginal, a special sensorium stretching from the deepest body-schema through the social and ideal selves and out into the world of peers, images and idols, making us able to reach, touch and feel into our social and temporal world. It is a phantom in the sense that it is an apparition, a body-double, a ghost-image, a neurological doppelgänger, a specifically dressed self-image in our sense of self. Thus, as we would suggest, the fashion phantom nudges us, pushes us towards into a world of desire (more than for example practical work wear). The fashion phantom is a "hungry ghost" of the soul; driving us to seek risk and the pleasures of social affirmation. It shines through when we are on top of ourselves, "beaming" with confidence (as Damasio has it), that assertive attitude that can seduce and grab another person's attention.

In resonance with Spinoza's idea of "conatus," by which "each thing, as far as it lies in itself, strives to persevere in its being,"[168] we are born with the need to thrive, and in order to thrive we need to be able to sense our environments and our sense of self within them. As we develop the capacity to perceive different types of inputs, our environments grow and we re-define our place within them through constant interaction, modulated by our cognition and abilities.[169] The world of fashion is one such environment, a world which has become all the more important and exploitative today as we are under continuous pressure to achieve and become more "ourselves" as a token of living at least the aesthetically pleasing version of a successful life.[170] So, just as there exists a common notion that the brain is a muscle that can be trained, just like our perception, the fashion phantom can be trained and attuned to its many imaginal "working environments." This is the many social cultures we appear in, from family and work, sports and dinners, to ceremonies and events, connecting deep down into the body-schema, unconsciously triggering emotions, such as arousal or blushing.

It is important to see that we all have fashion phantoms, as we are dressed most of our lives. Yet of course, we may have differently tuned and developed phantoms, just like we have different senses of self and bodies able to do different things. Just like we develop the self-image as a responsive sensibility to the world, anchored in our body through our enacted cognition, and a dancer's body-schema is attuned to the realm of dance, the fashion phantom is developed as we engage in the world of dress. Most of us have some minimal feelings of dance, or at least some rhythmic movement, and may still feel awkward if invited to a dance, while others love to dance, and you see it in the way they own their bodies in movement. In a similar vein, all of us live in clothes throughout our life, from being swaddled babies to the shrouding of our corpse, but we may still feel awkward if invited to a dress-party in a new setting or to join a scene we have little dressed training for, such as ceremonies in other cultures, or simply a friend's wedding. We thus cultivate the fashion phantom much like the other sensibilities we develop to grow a self: we train it in various settings, through pretend play, imagination, dreaming and browsing media, window shopping. But we challenge it by dressing up, playing with the attention of others, gambling for affirmation. We learn to see and to trust our senses, and if we are successful in the realm of dress, we learn to trust the sensibilities of our fashion phantom too; the phantom gets a clearer sense to us, an emotional silhouette, not unlike how the dancer develops proprioception and more elegant movements. Yet in some situations, dressing can still be like tightrope walking over an abyss of social uncertainty: we keep asking ourselves "how will my peers react?" and in our self-doubt we see every side look as a possible assault on our dressed precarity.

The fashion phantom is the part of the self which gambles with ideals, acting out through prosthetics, but simultaneously left vulnerable by these expeded limbs. The clash between desires, abilities and shared expectations can be felt when testing out the newest style, or challenging peers to wear that new look which still feels a bit too daring. It is the fashion phantom who imagines its new incarnation in those highly desired Ugg-boots, or tests its boundaries if that cheetah jacket can work amongst that group of friends, as in the earlier stories.

But the everyday gamble may also be unremarkable. As in the case of the lawyer at the conservative office, perhaps I seek a challenge to live out my fashion phantom. I challenge myself with wearing red socks one day. Slightly uncomfortable, yet thrilled, I test out the reactions of my peers. Some may give an approving look, affirming my bet, giving me a sense of pleasure, or perhaps the boss makes snarky remark and the gamble is over and I feel shamed.

But thanks to the shared ideals of certain fashion brands, I am not left out in the cold.[171] I pick the red socks from a brand I know my peers approve of. This may turn their initial scepticism into acceptance as I point out the socks are indeed from this or that desired Italian brand, and of the latest season or product "drop." The fashion phantom arms itself, building up defences through symbolic plays, learning to engage in self-defence, and it does so by staying up-to-date with the desires of my peers, sensing what gains their affirmation. But it can also do so through cultural playfulness, using irony and masks to learn play more successfully, and perhaps more dangerously. By developing my fashion phantom, I learn how to protect myself against humiliation, building a better social sensibility as well as self-esteem. Perhaps I seek more assuring alliances with brands and socially accepted markers, paying attention to the aspirations of my peers, while in other settings I do more high-risk gambling, exposing myself to the possibility of harsher judgments. The phantom in the body learns to play with its social prosthetics, moving more elegantly, perhaps gambling even more boldly.

Ghosts in the body

It is important to notice that we are not the first to think of the presence of "ghosts" or "phantoms" in the brain, and also that these concepts are not abstract or ethereal. It is a common concept amongst neuroscientists for understanding the images or maps we have of our bodies and the selves in the mind. As mentioned earlier, the body-schema of Damasio is a form of very concrete neural map of the body, a "ghost" in its most material sense.

The most famous of these ghosts is the phantom limb, the very physical emotion of pain from an amputated limb.[172] This is what is explored in neuroscientists Vilayanur Ramachandran and Sandra Blakeslee's famous book *Phantoms in the Brain*.[173] The phantom limb appears when a part of the body is amputated and the damaged sensory neurons from this area stops sending information to its designated area of the brain. However, there is no "silence" from the lost limb, instead, the brain perceives a neural limb in its place; a phantom. Primate studies have shown that after transection, a black hole in the sensory cortex develops corresponding to the sensory territory of the cut-off nerve. Soon following the transection (or repair) this area becomes occupied by substitute tactile input from adjacent hand areas that remain innervated by other nerves, something called cortical reorganization. When regenerating axons make peripheral connections, again there is a functional cortical reorganization. Sometimes this entails a total functional reorganization of the somatosensory cortex. Space in the brain is precious and every millimeter of it is used efficiently to help us survive. "Each neuron in the map is in a state of dynamic equilibrium with other adjacent neurons; its significance depends strongly on what other neurons in the vicinity are doing (or not doing)".[174] So with the death of the original neurons of the limb, the neurons beside it in the brain would reorganize to make use of the emptiness and thus a phantom limb appears to the mind. This implies that the nerves "speak" a new language to the brain, but also treats it differently on a material level.[175]

The implications to the studies of phantom limbs are staggering. First and foremost, the findings suggest that neural maps can change, sometimes with astonishing rapidity. This finding flatly contradicts one of the most widely accepted dogmas in neurology— the fixed nature of connections in the adult human brain. It had always been assumed that once this circuitry has been laid down in fetal life or in early infancy, there is very little one can do to modify it in adulthood. As Ramachandran and Blakeslee argues, "*Your own body* is a phantom, one that your brain has temporarily constructed purely for convenience."[176]

The plasticity of the interaction between body and mind in the example of phantom limbs also highlights how these processes of matching the "phantom" with the physical body is not always smooth. There are examples of a mismatch between the phantom in the body and otherwise healthy limbs. One such example can be the "xenomelia spectrum disorder" or "foreign limb syndrome," where a patient experiences a non-acceptance or rejection of one or more of his or her own extremities.[177] Xenomelia (from the Greek terms Xeno, "foreign," and Melos, "limb") points to an estrangement of one or more of one's limbs. At its worst, this may lead to self-inflicted amputation attempts.

A similar neuroplasticity of the self is tied to other types of ghosts and phantoms of the mind, from anorexia to the drifting body experience for some transgender people.[178] A commonly discussed version of a phantom body is in Body Dysmorphic Disorder (BDD), also known as dysmorphophobia, which is an example of what is sometimes also called "phantom fat" or "phantom fat syndrome."[179] People with BDD are convinced they look ugly or deformed, and become preoccupied with something about their physical appearance, obsessed with a detail or set of features they perceive as a flaw, even if that detail is not observable to others. It is a ghost seen only in their own perception. They may think, for example, that they have a large and "repulsive" nose, misshapen limbs, or severely scarred skin.[180] A formal diagnosis for anorexia entails a noticeable appearance deficiency whereas BDD patients may be obsessed with a distorted self-image that others cannot perceive, yet they are both related in their over reliance of a maladapted ghost-image of the self.[181]

With a drifting body experience, the person continuously checks the mirror, seeks compliments or reassurance from others, and is never secure enough to trust his or her own senses but is instead always mentally comparing themselves to other people. The patient experiences the "phantom body"[182] or "ghost" rather than his or her true appearance, thus affecting the feeling of attractiveness, which deeply affects the sense of self-esteem and self-worth.[183] In worse cases, the patients may stop seeing other people, work or socialize, become housebound, and in some cases even commit suicide. In the case of eating disorders, there may be an "anorexic ghost" in the body of the patient, a distorted experience of self-image which not only looks different in the mirror but feels different, not unlike the experience of a phantom limb.[184] The patent may be touching the body part or running the fingers over the body part to clinch the flesh or test for bumps and flaws, thus explicitly using touch to "feel out" the dysmorphic phantom. Even if thinness is the most commonly referenced form of dysmorphic body image, the opposite is also well-known, such as a bodybuilder extremely aware of diet and work-out routines, constantly tracking progress to address perceived flaws in body appearance.

We suggest the fashion phantom is another type of phantom of the brain; a socially cognitive ghost image of ourselves which connects the somatosensory body with the social sensorium - but it does so through the experience of dress. Throughout the social dressed realm, we cultivate a dressed self-image, a ghost-image of ourselves, how we imagine ourselves looking. Like the phantom in the body, this image may correlate with the actual image to various degrees, and we may update it every time we look in the mirror or see ourselves.

But the mirrored self-image is also affected by time and the trends: what aesthetic looks our peers aspire for. It is a ghost of its time: a doppelgänger of the Zeitgeist, located in our body. It is thus a self-image that is part real and part fantasy: *it is an image which connects the phantom of the mind with the phantasma of our collective fantasy of fashion*. It is this ghost image which relates to mimetic processes, which in turn are "clothed" in desire but also in high or low self-esteem and self-perception. As I look myself in the mirror, on my way to a date or job interview, eager to look my best, the look I seek, my ideal, is not static, but changes over time as the social dynamics of fashion changes together with the aesthetics of the times.[185]

The sensibility towards the dressed social realm evolves over time and in relation to the many waves of fashion, trends and identities a person lives though and enacts at various stages. Especially in adolescence we test many personas and use clothing to enter various scenes. We use a whole series of techniques and media to test how to interact with people and groups. It may be that we try out sports, and if we don't feel we fit in, we say "it was no fun," blaming the activity itself but we often mean we did not attune to the group of people in the team. We may use music styles and subcultures to meet other people, or activities in social organizations, from church to theatre, and in almost all these settings we also test various ways to dress, perhaps first to blend in, and later to test boundaries, impress or move up or beyond.[186]

Just like the other parts of the self, the fashion phantom is in a continuous feedback-loop, triangulating between self, socially enacted desires and what is mediated to us through our peers, idols and models; in clothing items, events, images, media and the phantasma of fashion in our shared social world. As the general trends evolve, so does our sensibility. A new hit song *feels* right for the time, and I share emotions with friends as we listen together, and it may grow to become an audible bond between us: dancing and singing it together may become very intimate and emotion laden.[187] Similarly, a new trend is *felt* in the body as a shared emotion, and our desires emerge in relation to our peers, as Oughourlian posits. But the fashion phantom also stretches out into the world, into the magical realm of idols and celebrities, the images, music, people, lifestyles that resonate with us: they resonate through our bodies as well as moves our social relationships, making us experience shared evolving emotions as they reverberate between us.

Here is where music and fashion overlaps in the way it moves bodies. Some tunes we listen to alone, while others just feel better sharing with others; they bring us together as we move, sing along, or dance together.[188] When we get it right, fashion connects to our social selves similar to how music moves our bodies and emotions together. At its best, fashion makes us experience the reverberating desires of our social relationships in ways we cannot experience alone or if not in tune with the times. It is a togetherness we cannot experience alone. In fashion, as in music, we dance alone, but together. We learn to use the "limbs" of garments and fashion to enhance our agency and pleasure. But we also learn to sense when we are not enough, how our dressed sense is not on par with what we hope it to be, or what we expect it to be in the eyes of our peers. As in dancing, the sync is related to both our peers and the overall timing.

Prosthetic fantasies

Much of our social and artistic techniques are part of our prosthetic culture; books can be extensions of our memory, and photos become archives as well as extensions of our senses: with their support we can capture fleeting moments, see inside bodies, examine planets far away and enhance our looks significantly. Prosthetics are thus both very technical and functional artifacts that are connected directly to our flesh to extend the shape of the body, but also more abstract cultural technologies which not only change and manipulate the extensions of the body but are altering our cognition, in the end both extending and manipulating our cognitive processes.[189] Clothing is such part of our body and sensorium, and we will see that fashion is an ephemeral and continually renewed prosthesis, enacting through our body on a physical as much as mental and social level. Thus we don't escape the real world through clothes or the "shallowness" of fashion, instead, we not only experience the world through clothes, but we sense and feel it's many physical as well as social forms.

Prostheses are only as powerful as their integration with our inner neural processes, our body image with its desires, thoughts, imaginations, and intentions, yet these processes also create a void, which our desires are eager and willing fill. The entity that emerges at this void, we call a phantom. The phantom is not a metaphysical dream, but a ghost which ties together our inner and outer worlds, inner and projected selves. And as we will argue further on, today, as fashion has become more and more prevalent in our everyday lives through images and media, it perpetuates a new gap in the world of clothes themselves.

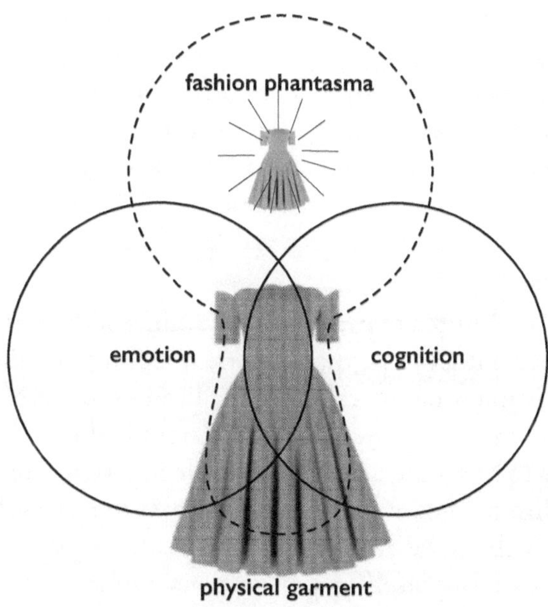

fashion phantasia;
imagination grounded in garment (but not filling them)
- animated through cognitive and emotive processes

To better frame the connection between the self-image and the collective imagination of fashion, it can be useful to draw parallels to the Greek roots to the word "phantom", as we usually connote ghost and phantom as unreal or irrelevant entities. However, the etymology suggests a much more imaginative yet still palpable nature of the phantom. In its Greek roots, the term *phantasia* was used as a mix of sensation (*aisthesis*) and opinion (*doxa*), and this differs highly from the Enlightenment obsession with Reality as a guardian of Truth, which in turn places images in relation to fancy, surface and illusion, and associates it with creativity rather than with knowledge. Our thinking today is a direct descendant of this blunt Enlightenment model: what is Real is True, and in opposition to this stands opinion, sensation, the image or "surface," which per definition is untrue.

But when it comes to sensation it's not that simple. Instead of this clear cut distinction between reality and imagination, the Greek emphasised how both sensation and opinion can simultaneously be both true and false, yet also definitely real, and such contradiction is a central component of the Greek idea of knowledge. Plato connects *aesthesis*, what appears, not only to *phantasia* but also to *episteme*, the word he uses for knowledge, and this is important, as aesthetics is thus not merely a shallow appearance, but a constitution of our shared reality, and this reality is not as easily divided into Real and unreal as we may like to think, but phantasia is part of our reality.[190] Images are constituent parts of the mind, producing real affects, actions, emotions and consequences.

We are cultured to perceive some realms of the socialized body as more important and real than others, weighting certain stimuli to point towards important cues about our lived experience. Nudity, for example, is shameful in some cultures and not in others. Similarly, pain is sometimes to be avoided at all costs, while in certain rites of passage, pain is the threshold over which one must pass to reach acknowledgement and growth. In the body-modification cultures pain is often a key ingredient, expressing itself in scarifications, tattoos and piercings all the way to full body suspension from meat hooks. In such cases, the pain is real even if induced with aesthetic or imaginary goals of *phantasia*; beauty, status and initiation. This reality of pain is affected by aesthetics.

As philosopher and cultural theorist Chiara Bottici highlights, Plato does not equate *phantasia* with a false unreality (or imagination) but on a parallel level to that of truth and knowledge; a knowledge tied to sensation. Also Aristotle pays attention to the coupled phantasm of mind and reality; "no one can learn or understand anything in the absence of sense, and when the mind is actively aware of anything it is necessarily aware of it along with an image (*phantasma*); for images (*phantasmata*) are like sensuous contents except in that they contain no matter."[191] Bottici traces *phantasma* to a crucial role in both cognition and action in Greek thought, as "*phantasmata* are not phantoms or specters. They are simple images without which even our most elementary mental operations would be impossible."[192] Similarly, *phantasia* is the basis for appetite, and Aristotle claims "there is no desiring without phantasia".[193] As Aristotle has it, phantasia is more than mere cognition, as it connects desire (*orexis*) with action (*praxis*).

The self-image is dressed and always in relation to the ideal me. Fashion binds together the external mediated world to our living fantasies and imaginations where we use stereotypes and images to mentalize, play, emotionalize, project and investigate possible paths of action. We may play with these images, and say we live a rich "inner life" of imagination, but it is an imagination that also takes place in and throughout the body. The fashion phantom thus connects the deeper layers and maps in our mind, the self and ideal self, and all the way out into the rich imagination of status symbols and rituals. The fashion phantom is a channel between the deep self and *fashion as a collective imaginary*, the aesthetic reality of *phantasia*, the ideological reality Bottici calls "the imaginal."[194]

Fashion is an imaginal world, and we live in it, for real, through our fashion phantoms. As a consumer I know the images in media and advertisement are arranged and photoshopped, yet they exist as phantasma in my mind as well as body, as cognitive constructs, social emotions felt throughout my body. Fashion as a phantasia is an image that lives like a mental model in my mind, even if I may not be able to consciously articulate it, I just know it "feels right."[195] And these images connect my desire (*orexis*) with my action (*praxis*) - and they live as schema in me: I may practice poses or dance steps in my room as a child, look at my own reflection in the window to examine my own posture, or throw a glance at myself in the mirror in the bathroom of a nightclub before meeting a date. In such cases I adapt behaviors, and I use inspirations I have gotten from the outside world as references to help me enact my desires and these postures are in my body.

Thus we must see fashion as much a bodily world as a social world because our social worlds are felt through our bodies. It is an embodied fantasy world that lives in our dreams and imaginations, but is of course also highly real, manifested in images, clothes, and emotions which are directly experienced by the body: it may seem "shallow," but it has real implications in our physical and biological lives. With the phantom in our brain we can reach out and touch the fantasies we have woven together with our peers and our shared imagination.[196]

Phantom limbs and amputated desires

On the level of self-image, we are continually drawn into struggles triggered by the discrepancies between our performance and our perception of performance. On an everyday basis, we may think we would perform well on a test and then fail, or imagine being in good shape, but then getting outperformed by peers. This happens all the time, and we continually update our self-image in relation to experiences and expectations.[197] But the discrepancies also trigger compensatory behaviors; we buy fancy things to boost a tarnished self-image, or comfort ourselves with sugar after a social bruise.[198] Goods are our predominant tokens in psychological self-regulation and symbolic self-completion. For example, we compensate our bad self-esteem in a job interview with getting a new suit, or modulate experiences of emotional dissociation with some "retail therapy" after a disagreement. The fashion phantom is thus anchored in our overall psychological well-being, and not merely in dress per se.

A fruitful way to grasp the fleeting world of fashion is through sociologist Zygmunt Bauman's point that fashion is a *perpetuum mobile*; a self-feeding, self-sustaining, self-propelling and self-invigorating process in permanent and principally unfinished revolution. Even if the expressions of fashion always change, little changes in its dynamic forces, and it cannot come to a halt, but rather seems to gain strength throughout our liberal and capitalist societies. As Bauman sees it, this is primarily because two contradictory urges clash violently to propel the machine; the compulsive longing to be part of a greater whole and simultaneous urge for individual uniqueness.[199] This contradictory craving for both security and freedom is even stronger today, Bauman argues, as our current configuration of society has made fashion into a dominant force for self-production. If earlier modernism offered many ways to manifest the self in the journey towards progress and emancipation, we today lack a utopia or idea of goal for our individual and collective journey. Instead, we live in a "hard, indomitable, menacing, and threatening reality [...] whose pressures must be obeyed."[200] Our lives no longer form a part of a collective struggle for shared improvement, but are instead turned towards individual survival, where "progress" has come to mean avoidance of being excluded. We no longer participate in grand projects, but have reduced our agency to be channeled through consumerism to mainly deal with the tinkering with our bodies and souls, and continually reinvent ourselves in order to stay attractive on the market of social lives, presenting ourselves as commodities on social media to stay popular and employable: job, identity, and recreation are all aesthetic projects in which we need to perform and achieve.

To Bauman, the tragedy is that this world is today's utopia; fashion is how the dream world of our desires presents itself today on a societal scale, yet it is a fantasy that is always at the risk of crumbling if not updated,

> "The odd idea of making uncertainty less daunting and happiness more permanent, steady and secure by continuous, uninterrupted changing one's ego, and changing one's ego by changing one's dresses, is the present-day reincarnation of utopia."[201]

There is no longer any reward in investing in long-term ideas of the future as the competitiveness in all social fields is in continuous flux, what Bauman calls the "liquid" tendencies of our time. This turns us as consumers into hunters. We are always chasing the latest difference, the latest demarcation that will bring us ahead; hunters driven forward like prey. And our desires dictate us so: we prefer the hunt to the capture. Thus this ceaseless hunt for the new is utopia itself, we love the chase and get quickly bored - and we fear our peers will get bored of us if we do not keep up. As Bauman sees it, fashion in this sense is not a hunt for a new utopia, a new state of bliss, but a ceaseless desire in the hunt itself; it is a utopia of no end.[202] In resonance with Caillios' corruption of play, fashion consumerism for Bauman is a corrupted hunt which has turned impossible to opt out of.

What Bauman points to is the uninterrupted movement of fashion and our desires, and how aggregated and individualized pressures to succeed in every sphere have made fashion a social game we are supposed to participate in, if not to win, then in order to escape the risk of exclusion. Our desires are continually updated in sync with the perpetuum mobile of fashion and its imaginal representations, as the fashion phantom keeps hunting the new possibilities for moving ahead, seeking affirmation and appreciation.

Through reinforcement, and over time, we learn that we are not enough: we are never ourselves enough to merge with our ideal self. Our peers challenge us to get that cheetah jacket, yet we are not courageous enough to accept the test, or a school friend questions the authenticity of our Ugg-boots, we learn that we live inside a shell which is under constant threat of breaking. A shell that is moldable and changeable, now more than ever, but also in need of protection. A shell that can cause us pleasure and pain, a shell that molds seamlessly into our physical experience of being in the world through the way it changes our body's posture and provides sensory input at every moment of our day.

In this way, we can sense how our body, clothed in unfashionable attire, is not only not enough, but also, it is not whole. If the looks from our peers echo empty of affirmation, we may also feel empty, as if our body lacks a social limb which we, just yesterday, could use to grab people's attention. Somatic markers in my body indicate *an amputation*, where my social limb would be, there is now *a void in my experience of self*. Amputated from the pleasurable sensations of draped silk on your skin, amputated from the proud, regal stance that your body assumes and the authoritative way your body moves when you wear your favorite pair of high heels, the way the jacket, tailored to your body, follows the curves you love and squeezes the areas that need adjustment, presenting to the world, a better you.

In correspondence with Girard's mimetic theory we will also always find new and better idols to compare ourself with, whose performance we desire to mirror, and our desires, as well as envy, is insatiable. And we don't seek feedback from just anyone, we seek exclusive connections and peers. The exclusive are drawn towards the exclusive. Connectivity is good, exclusivity is better.[203] And we will always find a lack in exclusivity, as elite prosthetics can always be better.

Thus our ideal self is never fulfilled, it is always producing new insatiable desires, hunting new competitive affirmations, and we sense this lack as we mirror ourselves on the desires of others, as Oughour-lian would argue. This produces a *void* in our self-image, a phantom limb, a sense of never fully being enough, but continually chasing after the sensation of emotional fulfillment. It is a void in our dreams, our ideal self, as much as a void in our physical experience of our self: the fashion phantom registers a discrepancy between ideal and reality.

In its continuous unfulfilled state of being, the fashion phantom suffers from a continuous phantom limb. I experience my self-image in a constant need to reach further into the cognitive realm of fashion, and I need the prosthesis to fill its void but also grasp and manifest who I want to be. The fashionable garment is an ephemeral prosthesis filling this deficiency between our desired image of self and my ideal phantasmata, my model me.

As a clinical term, a phantom limbs is a phenomenon in which amputees continue to feel the ghost of their pre-existing limb as if it was still there. These ghosts are often deformed or felt in other parts of their body. They can sometimes be moved, but are seldom in their owner's control.[204] In some cases, phantoms move like living, organic extensions coordinated with and to the body in both time and space. In other cases, they behaved autonomously, as if they had a will of their own, often with distressing consequences.[205]

In a similar vein, my experience of pain in the body affects my emotions but also my body-schema - the ghost image of myself in my body registers my pain and processes it to my consciousness.[206] Thus, as my self-image is hurt, I sense a similar pain as physical pain. This crucial emotion of self leads us to how fashion plays an important part of building social self-esteem, but also in the potential to undermine it. The broken heel or sudden ripped open crotch of the pants are social tears as well, the humiliation is inflicted on us and is hard to "heal" - even though there was no blood spilled. The pain is real.

Yet what are we to do with this emotional understanding of fashion? As with any new model of thought, it can help us see new things, as well as articulate and evaluate possible paths forward. It is our hope that if we think of fashion as a feeling, it can it help us rethink what fashion designers do and also help guide a transition towards more sustainable dress practices.

....

A woman in her 80s with a long career as a composer of classical music wears a wrinkled, skirt of limes, oranges, reds, yellows. She reveals that she has composed symphonies all over the world, but now that she's moved to New York, she is done with the black suits, neutral Ann Taylor blouses and long dark navy skirts of her profession. She moved to north Bronx to start fresh and had realized that no-one had ever written a travel guide to her new neighborhood. Along the way, she picked up a fluffy, yellow hat.

"I felt I needed *something else*. Something to take off from. A new opening."

Once she started wearing this yellow hat, people started giving her compliments.

"It felt like a Bronx thing."

She started wearing things towards the brighter end of the spectrum.

In the store, she buys a bright blue dress with elastic ruching on the side.

. . . .

"I want something red and colorful."

35, she says she is just getting over the death of her son. It's been two months and feels strange in black. She moves to the bright reds and tries on a silk Chinese (with the sideways buttons?) jacket, a deep purple hand-embroidered vest,

"I'm looking for something that calls to me."

. . . .

He has not been in the shop for some time. But today he returns with fresh enthusiasm and gets over to the work tables at once.

"I saw this great way of making exposed darts!"

He has brought two shirts, perhaps from his father, and gets on it at once. Without looking up, he measures, folds, pins and irons the shirts, accentuating the waist, running over to the mirror every time to get the darts where they should be. Next he concentrates at the machine. Last time he was in the shop he was mainly fooling around with his teen friends, so he needs a little help.

After a few photos in the mirror, he asks to have a photo with me in it too. Then he is back on his phone posting.

He leaves the shop dressed in one of his repurposed shirts, beaming.

TOWARDS SUSTAINABLE PHANTASIA

Today, we encounter fashion everywhere in our daily lives. Media is swamped by it, even newspapers have added special sections covering the latest trends, and the latest fashions seep into our social media feeds even if we are not interested in it. Fashion is like the news: even if we ignore directly reading about it, it is still everywhere. Fashion may be shallow, it may be fake, it may be real: it is a social reality with very real consequences. As we have argued, fashion is an emotional phenomenon that is embodied, and intimately connected to biological processes in the body, our cognition, and is in resonance with embodied social dynamics.[207]

This has consequences for how we work towards a more sustainable fashion system.So far, almost all answers to the overconsumption of cheap (and expensive) fashion has simply tried to make commodities less polluting through eco-cotton, recycling of materials and so on. It is hard to imagine fashion being something more or other than ready-to-wear goods, waiting for us in the storefront. It seems "sustainable fashion" can only be a slightly less bad version of what we see today. Perhaps one reason it seems so hard to change into more sustainable fashion practices is that most of us don't *know* fashion as much as we *feel* it. Changing our knowledge about the environmental impact of the industry does little to affect our behaviors, as the desires and feelings call us to buy anew.

So when, in 2015, fashion trend forecaster and authority Li Edelkoort turned to become yet another fashion guru proclaiming "the end of Fashion as we know it," and suggest ten reasons "why the fashion system is obsolete," she primarily posits how the current modus operandi of the fashion industry is in crisis. Similarly, and in resonance with Edelkoort, the magazine *Business of Fashion* asks if fashion trends even exist anymore, in a time where a "constant stream of 'newness' and an Instagram post can make a look go viral overnight."[208] Perhaps trends, as defined by marketing departments, trend forecasters and strategists, seem to lose their significance. But on the other hand, the industry keeps producing what fashion editor Michele Lee calls "McFashion," a type of fashion consumption just as unsatisfying, commonplace and utterly forgettable as the fast food equivalent.[209] The industry churns out ever larger amounts of garments, at cheaper prices, yet somehow the word Fashion still signals something consumers desperately desire; popularity, pleasure and likes, yet the cheap omnipresence of goods misses to signify anything special at all.[210]

But as we see it, it is not fashion per se that is in crisis, as much as the commodity-based model of fashion, and this *model of thought* may indeed be obsolete. The cultural and technological landscape in which fashion operates these days is also radically different than just a decade ago. At this moment at least, it seems the fashion industry has not yet caught up with how algorithms are programming what we see and read, and how this affects our desires. But also, algorithms do not necessarily help guide us towards more sustainable behaviors, or increase our general well-being - rather the opposite.[211]

The habitual way we think of fashion, based on a model of cultural industries, products, signification and semiotics, locks both consumers and the fashion industry into a killing loop. A loop that is based on infusing the fashion phantom with more and more energy, and deepening the void within ourselves, as felt in the hunger to keep whole. In the current inflation of cheap and accessible symbols, the exclusivity and monetary-based signification of fashion risk becoming as universal as it is obsolete.

What is desperately lacking are more sustainable imaginal worlds, ways of being with fashion that are more sustainable, on an environmental, social and psychological level. If we stop reducing fashion to be a concept defined by commodities, we may open some doors to how fashion could serve other purposes in our daily life and in society beyond the ready-to-wear market.

If we think of fashion as an emotion, we can find another way of understanding what fashion is and can be. By shifting the locus and agency of fashion, from the productive agency of the system to the emotional thrills of our bodies, we can possibly change the way consumers and designers think about and engage with fashion. As we challenge an unsustainable culture of consumerism we also ask how we might go beyond concepts like transparency, austerity and frugality, which unsuccessfully appeal to change consumer habits by trying to reason with them. If fashion instead is an emotion awoken in bodies, this changes the way we need to approach sustainability. Sustainable fashion has to be about changing the way we play.

Situating fashion as a sturggle within ourselves and our peers, can we create new systems for fashion, in its emotional, cognitive capacities, to move deeper into the abyss of the body? Deeper into the void within ourselves and thus into greater understanding of our desires and emotions? Perhaps the first step is for us to shine a light on the void in the human body, on which the fashion system operates, that is the fuel for its power.

If designers are to address a fashion in the body, they could be so much more than industrial production engineers. Designers could seek inspiration from doctors, psychotherapists or coaches, or hairdressers, masseurs, personal trainers, spiritual guides. What could be a fashion dietists? or a fashion doula? If fashion is not merely about producing fashionable goods, designers could help cultivate more healthy ways of being with the emotions of fashion. Yet the first step must be to better understand how fashion moves the body and plays with emotions, and find a language for this.

Then perhaps we can begin to think about how we might celebrate the ambiguous, complex, emotional, bold, imaginative self that fashionable people embody, the gamblers that excite our imagination. The feeling that fashion offers to deal with our emotions can be profound, when it comes to luxury items or even streetwear, their sensual, spiritual power helps the wearer to transcend the everyday. How can we each begin to develop this capacity to be fashionable, to access this depth of experience in local contexts? How can everyone be a fashionable person and play part in a fashionable community, a community of healing as much as adventure? How can we become self-aware of our ability to recognize and build around our own radiant light, and dare to risk our love?

If we shift our understanding of fashion from commodities to emotional play, could clothing be used to sense and articulate our emotions in different contexts? Could fashion be used to attune us to our own emotions, more consciously used as part of a journey towards self-discovery? Make us realize and come to terms with our cravings and anxieties? Maybe we can turn to real therapists, those who start with the person, and build both outwards and inwards. Can fashion design be a method to mix up the material, the cognitive, and the emotional in new ways to serve new purposes?

What kind of practices can we think of? We cannot know just yet. We have to test new ways to play.

And we have to feel it out.

1. The short narratives are collected encounters with fashion customers at a second hand clothing store in New York City, as well as part of interviews conducted in New York and Sweden between 2013-2018. Whereas most of the short stories/ cases are told by female subjects, this reflects how most of our interviewees were female, and they were also most open to share their stories. Most men's answers were clouded in rational language with a noteworthy silence about their feelings concerning dress choices, most often leaving out aesthetics as well as emotions. We leave to others to speculate about the causes of these differences, but it is important to see that embodiment happens in gendered, raced, abled bodies, not in "neutral" flesh. As pointed out by feminist scholar Elizabeth Grosz, bodies are "inscribed" by discourses and representational systems, imposing and enforcing regimes deeply onto bodies. (Grozs, Elizabeth (1995) *Space, time, and perversion: Essays on the politics of bodies*, New York: Routledge, p.33)

2. As noted by neuroscience researchers Steven Quartz and Anette Asp, humans are wired to compare and compete, something amplified by consumerism; "what makes modern consumption such a powerful force in our lives is that it builds on desires and motives that are etched very deep into our brains. In other words, it is part of our nature to consume. As we look into the ancient forces that shaped the modern brain and our consuming nature, we'll discover that like our closest genetic relative, the chimpanzee, we instinctively seek status." Quartz and Asp celebrate consumerism as the pinnacle of human culture, the fulfilment of our cultural biology, rather than a capitalist conspiracy stripping people from their natural happiness in unspoiled nature. The importance of their analysis is to highlight how the biological wirings in our being work in tandem with consumerism, that consumerism is not a fabricated need, but an amplification and harnessing of desires rooted deeply in our body, and in many ways, the fulfilment of these desires, for good and bad.. (Quartz, Steven & Anette Asp (2015) *Cool: How the brain's hidden quest for cool drives our economy and shapes our world*, New York: Farrar, Straus & Giroux, p.9)

3. The thrill of "play" we point to here should not be narrowed down to gambling experiences, such as in poker or roulette. Play is also a way to challenge and break repetition and form new patterns. As pointed out in Daniel Levintin's work on the emotional response to music, people who listen to music also experience "thrills

and chills" as the body processes the listening experience, activating brain regions thought to be involved in reward, motivation, and arousal - parts which play important role in pleasure and addiction. Pleasure and thrills can found in the violation of expectation, so common in music; "a sort of musical joke that we're all in on. Music breathes, speeds up, and slows down just as the real world does, and our cerebellum finds pleasure in adjusting itself to stay synchronized." (Levitin, Daniel (2007) *This is your brain on music*, New York: Plume/Penguin, p.191.)

4. Throughout this book we use a term "feel" in a broad sense, even though we generally subscribe to neuroscientist Antonio Damasio's distinction that emotions are primarily unconscious and bodily aspects, whereas feelings emerge in the conscious and can be symbolized and discussed. Emotions unfold on the stage of the body, whereas feelings take possession of the mind. Damasio combines emotions and feeling under the notion of affects;

> "Primary or universal emotions: happiness, sadness, fear, anger, surprise, disgust. Secondly or social emotions: embarrassment, jealousy, guilt, pride. Background emotions: wellbeing, malaise, calm, tension." (Damasio, Antonio (1999) *The feeling of what happens: body and emotion in the making of consciousness*, New York: Harcourt, p.51)

As we will unpack more later, in Damasio's view, consciousness does not emerge from language (or expressive thought), but comes into being as feelings emerge from our body and emotions, and these are later translated into language (thoughts).

Our suggested shift of the locus of fashion towards the body partly aligns with the "affective turn" in cultural studies and feminist theory, where affects and emotions unfold as contingent vital forces which resonate between objects and bodies, destabilizing and decentering self and body. Our focus is on the agency and emotions within the many-layered self and we try not to put emphasis on the contagious transmissions of affect. As we see it, unpacking the many-layered self and its gamble through fashion helps put the spotlight on how designers can utilize this embodied perspective in practice. We have found much resonance from a feminist understanding of the body (yet not all cited in this book), see for example: Braidotti, Rosi (1994) *Nomadic subjects: Embodiment and sexual difference in contemporary feminist theory*, New York: Columbia University Press; Clough, Patricia Ticineto and Jean O'Malley Halley, (eds) (2007) *The affective turn: Theorizing the social.* Durham: Duke University Press; Ahmed, Sara (2004) *The cultural politics of emotion*, Edinburgh: Edinburgh University Press, Blackman, Lisa (2012) *Immaterial bodies: affect, embodiment, mediation*, London: Sage ; and in relation to fashion theory, Parkins, Ilya (2008) "Building a Feminist Theory of Fashion: Karen Barad's Agential Realism." *Australian Feminist Studies* 23 (58): 501-515.

5. As most theorists of fashion suggests, all cultured bodies are shaped, adorned or embellished in some way, from haircuts, dress and make-up to muscled, groomed,

perfumed or purposefully ungroomed and unperfumed (as some fashions suggest). Fashion scholar Joanne Entwistle argues,

> "Dress is a basic fact of social life and this, according to anthropologists, is true to all known human cultures: all people 'dress' the body in some way, be it through clothing, tattooing, cosmetics or other forms of body painting. To put it another way, no culture leaves the body unadorned but adds to, embellishes, enhances or decorates the body." (Entwistle, Joanne (2015) *The Fashioned Body*, Cambridge: Polity, p.6)

6. In resonance with philosopher Jacques Ranciere's argument on the uneven distribution of the sensible, it is important to see that there is an uneven distribution of the fashionable (Ranciere, Jacques (2004) *The Politics of Aesthetics*, London: Continuum). Clothes and fashion have throughout the ages been heavily policed and used as a tool for separation, discrimination and oppression, to demarcate and enforce cultural as well as highly physical forms of violence, but also for struggles of sociopolitical as well as subjective liberation. Examples of this can be seen not least in Mama, Amina (1995) *Beyond the Masks: Race, Gender and Subjectivity*, London: Routledge, and lately in Tulloch, Carol (2016) *The birth of cool: style narratives of the African diaspora*, London: Bloomsbury.

7. Fashion is a prosthesis in the sense of an "auxiliary organ" for our shared aesthetic imagination. It is in resonance with Freud's statement that "with every tool man is perfecting his own organs, whether motor or sensory, or is removing the limits to their functioning [...] Man has, as it were, become a prosthetic god. When he puts on his auxiliary organs he is truly magnificent: but those organs have not grown on him and they still give him much trouble at times." (Freud, Sigmund (1930/1962) *Civilization and its discontents*, New York: W.W. Norton, p.42). We will discuss this more in detail in later chapters.

8. The prosthetic argument has a lot of overlap with fashion scholar Susan Kaiser's term "minding appearances" which she uses to bridge the Western mind/body disconnect and highlight the ambiguity and tension around dress practices that connect the biological body and style/fashion (as practice, culture and industry). As Kaiser argues,

> "The process of minding appearances is both embodied and material. The body itself, of course, is material (biological) and symbolic; indeed, it marks the intersections between the two, and can be described as the threshold of subjectivity" (p.79)

Kaiser continues,

> "Minding appearances enables the visual, embodied representation of who I am and who I am be-coming along with ideas, possibilities, ambivalences and anxieties with which I may find it difficult to grapple, much less resolve, in a verbal, linear, conscious manner. In this sense, appearance style becomes a

working model or a tentative truth claim about identity (i.e. who I am, who I am not, who I may be becoming). The process of minding appearance enables the construction of looks, as well as tentative understandings about the self in relation to others and consumer and media cultures, at a specific time and place." (p.80)

Susan Kaiser (2001) "Minding appearances: Style, truth, subjectivity," in Joanne Entwistle & Elizabeth Wilson (eds) *Body Dressing,* Oxford: Berg, p. 79–102.

9. Arnold, Rebecca (2001) *Fashion, Desire and Anxiety,* New Brunswick: Rutgers University Press, p.16. Quartz and Asp position their analysis of cool as a rebellion against petrified hierarchies, where "cool" signifiers and experience can bypass some of the walls between social strata. To Quartz and Asp, rebel cool acts

"as an oppositional force to bring down the traditional barriers to new life-styles, barriers that included racial and gender discrimination and social institutions designed to maintain the status quo. As oppositional cool consumption emerged, its new lifestyles diversified and expanded the routes to status, washing away the old hierarchical society of the 1950s, with its narrow conception of status, and replacing it with an increasingly pluralistic and diverse culture. The deeply entrenched idea that status is a fixed resource, and striving for it a zero-sum contest, turns out to be false. The diversifying, anti-hierarchical forces of cool consumption supply new status. For this reason, we'll suggest that the proliferation of consumer lifestyles over the last fifty years is best seen as a solution to the Status Dilemma." (Quartz & Asp, *Cool,* p. 19).

While this argument may ring true on a macro scale or in big metropolitan cities, it still leaves questions on group and inter-dividual levels and the hierarchies between different forms of "cool" in specific localities. Ask a youngster in school which brands and looks that count and you get a quick insight in how social pressures define aesthetic aspirations and the strict lines between inclusion and exclusion and which forms of "cool" which have no value at all.

10. Not all play is competitive, as play can also be cooperative, perhaps most famously exemplified in the Prisoner's Dilemma, where players act together to pursue a common goal and strive for mutual benefits through strategic interaction in turns. From a neurobiological perspective, the "social brain hypothesis" argues for how the relative size of the neocortex in primates correlates with how species engage in socially complex behavior and create cooperation and "we-thinking," such as coalitions, strategy development or, grooming clique size (Dunbar R. (1993) "Coevolution of neocortex size, group size and language in humans." *Behav. Brain Sci.* 16, p.681–735, - for a neuroscience perspective, see Rilling, J (2011) "The Social Brain in Interactive Games," in Todorov, A., Fiske, S., & Prentice, D. (Eds.) (2011) *Social neuroscience: Toward understanding the underpinnings of the social mind,* Oxford University Press, and also Engemann, D. A., Bzdok, D., Eickhoff, S. B., Vogeley,

K., & Schilbach, L. (2012). "Games people play—toward an enactive view of cooperation in social neuroscience." *Frontiers in Human Neuroscience*, 6, 148.

11. see for example the discussion on everyday anxieties in dress in Clarke, Alison,
and Daniel Miller (2002) "Fashion and anxiety." *Fashion Theory*, 6.2, p. 191-213.

12. Huizinga points out the dissemination and mutations of dress across time and
contexts, but also how especially male dress lost its profound playfulness, "There is
no more striking symptom of the decline of the play-factor than the disappearance
of everything imaginative, fanciful, fantastic from men's dress after the French Revolution.[...] This leveling down and democratization of men's fashion is far from
unimportant. The whole transformation of mind and society since the French Revolution is expressed in it." (Huizinga, Johan (1950) *Homo Ludens: A study of the
play-element in culture*, New York: Roy Publishers, p. 192f.)

13. Huizinga also emphasises that play forms factions, teams and groups, and sets
them against each other, yet within a boundaries of time and space, with its own
rules and order. Play is about the "formation of social groupings which tend to
surround themselves with secrecy and to stress their difference from the common
world by disguise or other means."

14. Caillois, Roger (1958/2001) *Man, Play and Games*, Urbana: University of Illi-
nois Press, p.59. Caillois argues for a specific typology of games: *Agon* (competition) rivalry between players, like in chess or a duel; *Alea* (chance), utilizing chance
to move the play but also raise stakes, like in dice; *Mimicry* (mimesis), pretend play,
like in theatre or role playing; *Ilinx* (vertigo), altering perception through disorien-
tation, but also physical thrill of risk-taking, like in roller coasters. It is important
to notice that Caillois does not set games as a lighthearted or trivial activity, but are
at the core of human relationships and sometimes with deadly consequences. For
example, as in the case of competition (Agon), rivalries are settled by the function
of games, such as in the tournament or duel, and the so-called courtly war - its
purpose is to set the agonists under equal rules, "so that in return the victor's supe-
riority will be beyond dispute." (p.15)

15. Caillois, *Man, Play and Games*, p.5f.

16. Caillois continues, "Wearing a mask permits Dionysian societies to reincarnate
(and feel imbued with) powers and spirits, special energies and gods. It covers a
primitive type of culture founded, as has been shown, on powerful association of
pantomime with ecstacy. Spread over the entire surface of the planet, it seems to be
a false solution, obligatory and fascinating, prior to slow, painful, deliberate, and
decisive social progress. The birth of civilization means the emergence from this
impasse." (p.99)

17. As Caillois argues, there has to be some latitude for player initiative and room for
uncertainty. If there is no element of challenge, uncertainty, instability and risk, the
game loses its purpose. "An outcome known in advance, with no possibility of error

or surprise, clearly leading to an inescapable result, is incompatible with the nature of play." (p. 7)

18. The emotional intensity of fashion happens in the everyday, in the hallways, in the glances and faces of social interaction as we decide to gamble with our appearance. Placing a risk that we may get rejected and hoping for not only appreciation, but praise, fashion is a thill, a powerful yet often unnoticed rush, that happens in our bodies in relation to the immediate social environment. The risk is played out against the possibility of shame and humiliation, a felt experience of the power of social pain and the discovery that social rejection or exclusion "social pain" is processed by some of the same neural regions that process physical pain - but the memories of shame stick longer to our self-image and self-esteem (Eisenberger, Naomi I., Matthew D. Lieberman, and Kipling D. Williams (2003) "Does rejection hurt? An fMRI study of social exclusion." *Science,* 302.5643, pp.290-292.; Eisenberger, Naomi I., and Matthew D. Lieberman (2004) "Why rejection hurts: a common neural alarm system for physical and social pain." *Trends in cognitive sciences,* 8.7, pp.294-300.; MacDonald, Geoff, and Mark R. Leary (2005) "Why does social exclusion hurt? The relationship between social and physical pain." *Psychological bulletin,* 131.2.)

This means our taste and style of clothing is a result of direct, immediate ridicule or praise about an article of clothing on our bodies. These are the instances that stick closest in our emotional memories, and the style of our clothes play an active part in these emotionally charged situations. This resonates with Nigel Thrift's notion on style as having an agency of itself in social relationships, what he calls the "technologies of glamour,"

> "style does not consist of a list of factors that have to be ticked off, nor does it constitute a totality of meaning. *Style is a modification of being that produces captivation, in part through our own explorations of it.* Style wants us to love it and we want to be charmed by it; we want to emulate it, we want to be definite about it, we want to be absorbed by it, we want to lend ourselves to what it has become. Style, in other words, can be counted as an agent in its own right in that it defines what is at issue in the world that we can engage with." (Thrift, Nigel (2010) "Understanding the material practices of glamour," in Melissa Gregg & Gregory Seigworth (eds) *The Affect Theory Reader*, Durham: Duke University Press, p.297.)

19. As Caillois writes,

> "In the confused, inextricable universe of real, human relationships, on the one hand, the action of given principles is never isolated, sovereign, or limited in advance. It entails inevitable consequences and possesses a natural propensity for good or evil. In both cases, however, the same qualities can be identified: *The need to prove one's superiority; The desire to challenge, make a record, or merely overcome an obstacle; The hope for and the pursuit of the favor of destiny;*

Pleasure in secrecy, make-believe, or disguise; Fear or inspiring fear [...]" Caillois, *Man, Play and Games*, p.64f.

20. The mask, the carnivalesque, breaks through convention, and "characterizes equivocally sensual intrigues and mysterious plots against powers that be. It is the symbol of amorous or political intrigue. It is disturbing and somewhat of a thrill. At the same time, it assures anonymity, protects, and liberates. At a ball, it is not merely two strangers who hold and dance with each other; they are two beings who symbolize mystery and who are already bound by a tacit promise of secrecy. The mask ostensibly liberates them from social constraints. [...] The entire intrigue is conducted like a game, i.e. conforming to pre-established conventions, in an atmosphere and within limits that separate it from and do not entail and consequences for ordinary life." (Caillois, *Man, Play and Games*, p.130f.

21. Play is a social interaction that can emerge between two or more autonomous agents who mutually regulate a dynamic coupling through "participatory sense-making." In accordance to Ezequiel Di Paolo and Hanne De Jaegher's "Interactive brain hypothesis," such coupling denotes two systems through which the states in one of them have a functional dependence on the state variables of the other, which may be non-linear and time-varying (what they call "dynamical" coupling). For example, in play, the roles and contexts may change during interactions, e.g. one player can trust a peer in one round, but have to see through the deception the next round, and furthermore enact and coordinate these beliefs into a dynamic strategy of interaction to play better. See Ezequiel Di Paolo and Hanne De Jaegher (2012) "The interactive brain hypothesis," *Front. Hum. Neurosci.*, June 2012, 6: 163.

22. Howard, John C. (1996) "Shopping to cope with stress: A study of therapeutic play," Dissertation, Pennsylvania State University, p.37f

23. Geertz, Clifford (1973) *The Interpretation of Cultures*. New York: Basic Books.

24. Howard (1996) "Shopping to cope with stress", p.38.

25. Howard (1996) "Shopping to cope with stress", p.68.

26. As Caillois warns,

> "Now competition is nothing but a law of nature. In society it resumes its original brutality, as soon as it finds a loophole in the system of moral, social, and legal constraints, which have limits and conventions comparable to those of play. That is why mad, obsessive ambition, applied to any domain in which the rules of the game and free play are not respected, must be denounced as a clear deviation which in this case restores the original situation." (p. 46)

The same can happen to mimicry:

> "It is produced when simulation is no longer accepted as such, when the one who is disguised believes that his role, travesty, or mask is real. He no longer

plays another. Persuaded that he is the other, he behaves as if he were, forgetting his own self. The loss of his real identity is a punishment for his inability to be content with merely playing a strange personality. It is properly called *alienation*." (p.49)

27. Proprioception is a central ability trained by dancers and musicians who not only need high proprioception for enhanced posture and performance, but also to avoid injury. (see for example Smitt, M.S. & H.A. Bird (2013) "Measuring and enhancing proprioception in musicians and dancers" Clinical Rheumatology 32.4: 469–473, and also Leanderson J, Eriksson E, Nilsson C & Wykman A (1996) "Proprioception in classical ballet dancers. A prospective study of the influence of an ankle sprain on proprioception in the ankle joint." American Journal of Sports Medicine, 24(3):370-4.)

28. Author Rob Walker calls our current commodity belief system "murketing", a mix of "murky" and "marketing." His term exposes how marketing is not so much propaganda as much as a murky language, tweaking our attention, used by consumers as much as abused by brands. Brands help consumers make sense of the world, they orient social relations and hierarchies, and users also contribute to their reproduction (in reviews, gossip, etc) (Walker, Rob (2008) *Buying In: The Secret Dialogue Between What We Buy and Who We Are*, Random House) - Neuromarketing guru Martin Lindstrom similarly draws strong similarities between the production of religious rituals and marketing as a way to get brands to "stick" in the lives of the consumer (Lindstrom, Martin (2008) *Buyology: Truth and Lies About Why We Buy*, New York: Doubleday)

29. Pirsig, Robert (1974) *Zen and the Art of Motorcycle Maintenance*, New York: Harpertorch : p.267

30. Bechara, A., Damasio, A. R., Damasio, H., & Anderson, S. W. (1994). Insensitivity to future consequences following damage to human prefrontal cortex. *Cognition*, 50(1-3), 7-15.

31. A simple definition of fashion is that of journalist Susanne Pagold; "to look like everyone else, but before everyone else." (Pagold, Suzanne (2000) *De Långas Sammansvärjning*. Stockholm: Bonniers: p.8) The "everyone else" Pagold refers to made more sense when there still was a "mainstream" and fashion would "dictate" looks, but we still find this definition useful as it puts emphasis on the social and temporal aspects of certain forms of popular dress and that there is a central *competitive* element in fashion: *to be among the first*, and thus differ from those we consider are like "everyone else."

32. Another way to highlight the two poles on the continuum between clothes and fashion is that clothes are more individual, concern the wearer's body and environment, whereas fashion is a collective and shared desire, that is, fashion needs to be social, it can never be individual. However, this is not to say that clothes are more

"inside" us (or more "authentic") and fashion is "outside" us in the social realm (and thus "inauthentic"). Fashion is more "charged" by the energy of the moment, by our shared desires, and this charge is lost over time, thus old garments which once felt "of the moment" lose their energy and become "mere" garments. Yet both poles of the continuum are experienced in and through our bodies, tying together the imaginal realm with our embodied cognition.

33. The metaphor of thinking clothes as a second skin has a long history, not least explored in Marilyn Horn (1969) *The Second Skin, An Interdisciplinary Study of Clothing Horn*, Boston: Houghton Mifflin, and in Kirsty Dunseath's (ed) collection of essays (1999) *Second Skin: Women Write about Clothes*, London: Women's Press. It is important to also notice that "skin" in all its forms is used to sort, delineate and discriminate, see Fanon, Frantz (1967) *Black Skin, White Masks*, New York: Grove Press, but also hooks, bell (1990), *Yearning: Race, Gender, and Cultural Politics*, Boston: SouthEnd Press.

34. Entwistle's pioneering work on fashion embodiment points to this very clearly,

> "Dress does not merely serve to protect our modesty and does not simply reflect a natural body or, for that matter, a given identity; it embellishes the body, the materials commonly used adding a whole array of meanings to the body that would otherwise not be there. While the social world normally demands that we appear dressed, what constitutes "dress" varies from culture to culture and also within a culture, since what is considered appropriate dress will vary according to the situation or occasion." (Entwistle, Joanne (2000) "Fashion and the Fleshy Body: Dress as Embodied Practice," *Fashion Theory*, 4(3),p.324)

35. Tensions around religious dress are obvious in many of today's societal conflicts, especially around what is considered "modest" wear. But, as fashion scholar Elizabeth Wilson highlights, clothes mark an ambiguous boundary between the biological body and the social world, and the regulation of dress has played an explicit part of the modern project. Thas been apparent, not least concerning the modulations of meanings in dress which has affected the boundaries of labor, leisure, the social control of public and private spheres, and not least sexuality and gender. Wilson, Elizabeth (1985) *Adorned in dreams: fashion and modernity*, London: Virago.

36. It is easy to miss the skin's role in perception. The cutaneous senses include touch and everything else we feel through our skin: temperature, texture, pressure, vibration, pain, itch information, yet when we think of "touch" amongst our senses we usually think of the hands and fingers. Yet, as posited by Morrison et al, the skin is the site of events more than a membrane, but an organ which processes our interaction with one another, and through which we feel social interactions. Touch can mediate social perceptions, but also skin responses, the feeling of pain etc, responds to emotional states and events. (Morrison, I, Löken, L. S., & Olausson, H. (2010) "The skin as a social organ." *Experimental brain research*, 204(3), 305-314.

37. As Entwistle suggests, "the dressed body is a fleshy, phenomenological entity that is so much a part of our experience of the social world, so thoroughly embedded within the micro-dynamics of social order, as to be entirely taken for granted." (Entwistle, "Fashion and the Fleshy Body," p.327) An example can be the micro-dynamics of touch, or of the erotic charge of touch and gloves, as can be seen in the movie *Carol* (2015) where the shop attendant Therese Belivet (Rooney Mara) spots the beautiful, elegant Carol (Cate Blanchett) in a 1950s Manhattan department store. But it is Carol's act of "forgetting" her gloves at the counter which serves as a material link between their desires, a detail which also carries the riskful promise of (the forbidden) touch.

38. Assemblage is a term used by French philosophers Gilles Deleuze and Felix Guattari to capture how our bodies "co-function" with materials, environment or other bodies: like a symbiosis it is a matching of components into an emergent whole. The part retain their autonomy, but as the density of connections intensifies the parts form a unit which enters higher "level of organization" (such as cells, individual organs, individual organism). (see DeLanda, Manuel (2016) *Assemblage Theory*, Edinburgh: University of Edinburgh Press)

39. Gopnik, Adam (2016) "Feel Me: What the new science of touch says about ourselves," *The New Yorker*, May 16, 2016, pp.56-66.

40. Made up of mechanoreceptors, thermoreceptors, pain receptors, and proprioceptors

41. All it took was a few seconds of holding a warm cup of coffee in an elevator for study participants to rate a written person's personality as more generous, more social, happier, and better natured, compared to those who held an iced coffee for the same few seconds. Also, in a study in which participants held a hot therapeutic pad or a cold pad and were given the option of keeping or giving their reward to a friend, those who held the hot pad were more likely to give their gift away. Williams, Lawrence E., & Bargh, John A. (2008). Experiencing physical warmth promotes interpersonal warmth. *Science*, 322(5901), 606-607.

42. One study, for example, showed that posing for one minute in a high-power stance, where the subject impersonated a powerful posture, led to increases in testosterone, decreases in cortisol, and increased feelings of power and tolerance for risk. Specifically, 86% of high-power posers took a gambling risk that would result in high rewards compared to 60% of low-power posers. (Carney, D., Cuddy, A., & Yap, A. (2010). Power Posing: Brief Nonverbal Displays Affect Neuroendocrine Levels and Risk Tolerance. *Psychological Science*, 21(10), 1363-1368.

43. Our cognition is like a blind person tapping around with a stick, that "bring[s] forth" objects to the senses (Varela et al 1991). Through a process of probing and systematic movement engaging many senses and motor-skills at once, the world is "co-determined in a form of negotiation between organism and environment". Ac-

cording to Damasio, emotions are rooted in patterns of visceral sensations that occur in our bodies as reactions to a situation (Damasio, Antonio (2003) *Looking for Spinoza : Joy, sorrow, and the feeling brain,* Orlando, Fla.: Harcourt). These physiological processes mostly occur at imperceptible levels, without our conscious knowledge, at this point, they are called somatic markers, but when various processes become associated and strong enough to reach our busy conscious minds, we identify these as feelings. The neural basis of these patterns occurs through repeated stimulation, which forms efficient pathways of information at the neural level, forming associations between our perceived situation or environment, the movement of chemical and electric activation of neurons in our bodies, and the action we need to take to survive such that the actions become more automatic. At the neural level, these patterns and associations form through Hebbian learning, a phenomenon in which simultaneous activation of neurons lead them to undergo some growth process or metabolic change that results in more efficient activation. It's the idea that neurons that fire together, wire together (Lowel, S., and W. Singer. "Selection of Intrinsic Horizontal Connections in the Visual Cortex by Correlated Neuronal Activity." *Science,* 10 Jan. 1992.) In the enactivist tradition, Alva Noe argues that when we think of perception it is touch we should model our understanding from, not vision. (Noe, Alva (2004) *Action in Perception,* Cambridge: MIT Press) That is, we don't "take in" reality passively, like light streaming into our eyes, but our perception is an active process of feeling out the world. As Noe puts it, "What we perceive is determined by what we do (or what we know how to do); it is determined by what we are ready to do. [...] we enact our perceptual experience; we act it out." (Noe 2004: 1) We often engage our whole bodies in the act of perception, we bend our heads, squint our eyes, turn towards the source of a sound, cup our hands behind our ears, we search and probe with our hands, sniff and taste - and also our skin is part of this activity.

44. There are of course radical differences between Plato's world view and contemporary neuroscience, yet Plato's emphasis on aesthetics and imagery as a sensory tool for knowledge overlaps with many views today. For example, Varela et al see cognition as an ongoing capacity for sensual interaction with the world, of "having a world," as they say (Varela, F.J. (1991) "Perception and the origin of cognition" In Varela & Dupuy (eds) *Understanding Origins,* Boston: Kluwer, p.150). This understanding is a move "away from the idea of a world as independent and extrinsic to the idea of a world inseparable from the structure of these processes of self-modification" which they instead see as "rooted in the structures of our biological embodiment, but are lived and experiences within the domain of consensual action and cultural history" (ibid: 139). This in turn resonates with the idea of *phantasma* as cognitive tools and models of "having a world."

45. Lakoff, George & Mark Johnson (1999) *Philosophy in the flesh: the embodied mind and its challenge to Western thought,* New York: Basic Books; Pfeifer, Rolf, and Josh

Bongard (2006) *How the body shapes the way we think: a new view of intelligence.* Cambridge: MIT press.

46. Philosopher Maurice Merleau-Ponty aims is to "re-establish the roots of the mind in its body and in its world, going against the doctrines which treat perception as a simple result of the action of external things on our body as well as against those which insist on the autonomy of consciousness [...] Far from being merely an instrument or object in the world our bodies are what give us our expression in the world, the visible form of our intentions" (Merleau-Ponty, Maurice (1976) *The Primacy of Perception,* Evanston: Northwestern University Press, p3ff)

47. Even if Merleau-Ponty puts emphasis on the body, he still sometimes uses metaphors of the body as a vessel or container of being, for example the body as the "vehicle of being in the world," while more contemporary theorists of embodiment try to avoid such metaphors to highlight the non-dualism between body and being (Merleau-Ponty, Maurice (1981) *The Phenomenology of Perception,* London: Routledge, p.82.)

48. Cultural factors, such as our concepts for being in the world, help configure our lived sociobiological functions. For example, sexual drive, based in the biological domain, still expresses itself through many cultural forms, as does selection and aggression: we are in the world through these embodied concepts and the material manifestations they bring along. John Berger argues in *Ways of Seeing* (London: Penguin, 1972) a difference between the naked and nude, where the latter is a nakedness dressed in social convention. Anne Hollander argued along similar lines in *Seeing Through Clothes* (New York: Viking, 1978) to show how different fashions throughout the ages also affected the way painters drew the nude body as proportioned in accordance to the clothing ideals of the time. Lakoff and Johnson suggests a socio-biological approach to thinking and philosophy, to help reveal "what we understand the world to be like is determined by many things: our sensory organs, our ability to move and manipulate objects, the detailed structure of our brain, our culture, and our interactions in the environment, at the very least." (Lakoff & Johnson, *Philosophy in the flesh,* p.102)

49. For example, students treat teachers differently depending if he or she wears formal as opposed to casual clothes (see for example Behling, D. U., & Williams, E. A. (1991) "Influence of dress on perception of intelligence and expectations of scholastic achievement." *Clothing and Textiles Research Journal,* 9, pp.1–7. as well as Morris, T. L., Gorham, J., Cohen, S. H., & Huffman, D. (1996) "Fashion in the classroom: Effects of attire on student perceptions of instructors in college classes." *Communication Education,* 45, pp.135–148.) Similarly, women wearing masculine clothing in job interviews are more likely to get the job (Forsythe, S. M. (1990) "Effect of applicant's clothing on interviewer's decision to hire." *Journal of Applied Social Psychology,* 20, pp.1579–1595.), whereas women may be seen as unprofessional if dressing too sexy in prestigious positions (Glick, P., Larsen, S., Johnson,

C., & Branstiter, H. (2005) "Evaluations of sexy women in low-and high-status jobs," *Psychology of women quarterly,* 29(4), pp.389-395.)

50. In a famous study investigating deindividuation, found that subjects who were hoods and capes administered electric shocks to those posing as prisoners for twice as long as those who wore name badges (Haney, C., Banks, C., and Zimbardo, P. G. (1973) Interpersonal dynamics in a simulated prison. Intern. J. Criminol. Penal., 1,69-97). In the same scenario, subjects who wore nurse uniforms were less aggressive in administering shocks than those not wearing uniforms. (Johnson, R., & Downing, L. (1979). Deindividuation and Valence of Cues: Effects on Prosocial and Antisocial Behavior. *Journal of Personality and Social Psychology,* 37(9), 1532-1538).

51. A study found that wearing a bikini makes women feel ashamed, eat less, and perform worse at math (Fredrickson, B. L., Roberts, T., Noll, S. M., Quinn, D. M., & Twenge, J. M. (1998) "That swimsuit becomes you: Sex differences in self-objectification, restrained eating and math performance," *Journal of Personality and Social Psychology,* 75, pp.269–284.)

52. But this mismatch can also happen in the details, or on a very small part of a garment, and it may still cause emotional harm. For example, if I get a stain on my white pants, and I have a memory of shame connected to that, I sense an amputation, and my pants no longer "work." Entwistle posits as example in resonance with this:

> "Dress is part of the presentation of self; idea of embarrassment and stigma play an important part in the ways in which dress has to 'manage' these as well as the way dress may sometimes be the source of our shame. However, the ridicule is not simply that of personal faux pas, but the shame of failing to meet the standards required of one by the moral order of the social space. A commonly cited dream for many people is the experience of suddenly finding oneself naked in a public place: dress, or the lack of it in this case, serves as a metaphor for feelings of shame, embarrassment and vulnerability in our culture as well as indicating the way in which the moral order demands that the body be covered in some way." (Entwistle, Joanne (2015) *The fashioned body: fashion, dress and modern social theory,* Cambridge: Polity Press, p.35)

53. In many cases with sports teams, hazing is used to reify homonormative dress, or when "ridicule" in a fraternity often involves dressing the subject in women's dress.

54. Adam, Hajo & Adam Galinsky (2012) "Enclothed cognition", *Journal of Experimental Social Psychology,* 48, pp.918–925. Adam & Galinsky's ideas were later supported by another study on the effects of clothing on working memory capacity (WMC), see Van Stockum, Charles & Marci DeCaro (2014) "Enclothed Cognition and Controlled Attention During Insight Problem-Solving," *Journal of Problem Solving,* Vol 7, pp.73-83.

55. For example, people who carry a heavy clipboard change their judgment of importance, with the property of weight translating into the "weight" of their position, boosting their ego (Jostman, N. B., Lakens, D., & Schubert, T. W. (2009) "Weight as an embodiment of importance," *Psychological Science*, 20, pp.1169–1174.)

56. Adam & Galinsky "Enclothed cognition", p.919.

57. Using the term prosthetic, we point towards the auxiliary organ fashion provides at the intersection of our body and our social desires. Its use does not emerge from a wounded, scarred or disabled body, but it is important to see it is a body stuck in an asymmetrical relationship to the aspirations of its wearer and peers: it is always affected by what is currently considered a fashionable (and habitual) "wholeness." (see more on this in later sections)

58. Studies have shown that the mood of the user changes with trying on unfamiliar or new clothes, both in a positive or negative way. (Moody, Wendy, Peter Kinderman, and Pammi Sinha (2010) "An exploratory study: Relationships between trying on clothing, mood, emotion, personality and clothing preference." *Journal of Fashion Marketing and Management*, 14.1, pp.161-179. Also social psychologist Karen Pine has also argued for a link between mood and clothing, for example how depressed women are more likely to wear jeans, and how women are stressed women narrows down their options for what to wear, using less of their wardrobe, in fact neglecting as much as 90 percent of it. Thus clothes not only express how we feel but also play an active role in affecting how we feel. This leads Pine to argue that clothes could possibly be used to address mood-swings if not depression. (Pine, Karen (2014) *Mind What You Wear: The Psychology of Fashion*, Kindle Single)

59. Entwistle explicitly argues for clothes as orientation, when she reminds,

> "Dress is always located spatially and temporally: when getting dressed one orientates oneself/body to the situation, acting in particular ways upon the surfaces of the body in ways that are likely to fit within the established norms of that situation. Thus the dressed body is not a passive object, acted upon by social forces, but actively produced through particular, routine and mundane practices. Moreover, our experience of the body is not as inert object but as the envelope of our being, the site for our articulation of self." (Entwistle, "Fashion and the Fleshy Body," p.335)

See also feminist scholar Sara Ahmed's discussion on the "orientation" of matter and bodies, that matter aligns our actions with the intentions of the design, a simple example may be that if there is a chair in a room we are "drawn" to go and sit on it: it orients my body towards the posture of sitting. (Ahmed, Sara (2010) "Orientations matter," in Diana Coole and Samantha Frost (eds) *New materialisms: ontology, agency, and politics*, Durham: Duke University Press)

60. Damasio suggests *orientation* is a central trope in the process of tying together neural maps with the sense of self in the mind;

> "The sense of self introduces, within the mental level of processing, the notion that all the current activities represented in brain and mind pertain to a single organism whose auto-preservation needs are the basic cause of most events currently represented. The sense of self orients the mental planning process toward the satisfaction of those needs. That orientation is only possible because feelings are integral to the cluster of operations that constitutes the sense of self, and because feelings are continuously generating, within the mind, a *concern* for the organism." (Damasio, *Looking for Spinoza*, p.208)

61. As Crawford notices, the "normal" does not mean natural or unmanipulated as every human culture forms bodies according to normative ideals. (Crawford *Phantom limb*, p.3ff)

62. An example can be the para-athlete and model Aimee Mullins and her cheetah/blade running legs, or her McQueen prosthetics legs (Mullins TED-talk "My 12 pairs of legs" available at: https://www.ted.com/talks/aimee_mullins_prosthetic_aesthetics)

63. This resonates with Mark Seltzer's notion of the "double logic of prosthesis," the simultaneous self-extension and self-cancellation/mutilation of body and agency. Studying how Henry Ford rationalized the production line and minimized human workers to formulas of relevant parts, in name of supporting "substandard men" to perform expected and repeated labor in the mass-standardized products, labor and body identities as well as consumers. (Seltzer, Mark (1992) *Bodies and Machines*, London: Routledge.) A similar situation may appear as models and athletes become models for prosthetics, creating new expectations on the "supercrip" not only overcoming the limits of the body and the impairments of society, but also raising the standard for subjects with access, resulting in self-cancellation of abilities. See more in Hamraie, Aimi (2017) *Builing access: Universal design and the politics of disbility*, Minneapolis: University of Minessota Press.

64. Parallels can be drawn to how Katherine Hayles points out how media is pushing the agency of the human into an amplified realm, beyond the human, intensifying, subjectifying and replacing our senses. Prosthesis is a form of media, not bound by the limits of the human, or merely "filling" in a void on the level of the human: it is more-than-human (post-human). (Haynes, Katherine (1999) *How we became posthuman: virtual bodies in cybernetics, literature, and informatics*, Chicago: Chicago University Press.) For a more in-depth discussion on the amalgamation of biology and media, see Thacker, Eugene (2004) *Biomedia*, Minneapolis: University of Minnesota Press.

65. Crawford, Cassandra (2014) *Phantom limb: Amputation, embodiment, and prosthetic technology.* New York: NYU Press, p. 8.

66. Olesen, Virginia (1992) "Extraordinary events and mundane ailments: The contextual dialectics of the embodied self," in Ellis & Flaherty (eds) *Investigating subjectivity: Research on lived experience*, Newbury Park: Sage.

67. As Crawford highlights, ""relocated in the brains rather than the minds of amputees, the phantom was rendered biomedical 'real,' factual, and authentic rather than fictions, fraudulent, and fanciful. Equally notable, however, was the reconceptualization of prostheses. Because of the neuroscientific research on phantom limb syndrome, artificial limbs became key to appreciating, preventing, and/or harnessing the capacity of the human cortex to reorganize itself." (Crawford *Phantom limb*, p.13) The focus of the studies of prosthetics has thus moved from absence to synergy.

68. In this sense the prosthetics of clothing acts like the "extended mind" in social cognition:

> "With a model of an extended mind we have to change our definition of what we class as a mind. It is no longer just the grey matter inside our skulls. It extends beyond our skin and includes the things we interact with and the environments that surround us. These can be of our own making as in niche constructions. Our minds are as much the cups we drink from as the chair we sit on and the neurons firing in our brains when we perform these actions. Minds are not just about being rational in our approach to others but also relational in a truly social sense. Our social cognition is therefore not only to be found on the prefrontal and temporal cortex where memories and information about others is located. It is also to be found in the accumulation of artifacts, their shape, touch, taste and smell. In that sense our social cognition is distributed throughout the world we live in, a basic part of the niche we have built." (Gamble, Clive, John Gowlett & Robin Dunbar (2014) *Thinking big: how the evolution of social life shaped the human mind*, London: Thames & Hudson, p.107)

69. As discussed in the research by Kat Jungnickel, the introduction of pockets into women's clothes coincided with the women's emancipation at the end of Victorian times. The bloomer pants was another design which enhanced the movement and activities of women in public space (such as biking). On another note, the last decades have seen new developments of carrying systems, strapped to the body. Examples can be backpacks and babycarriers, which shift the weight from the shoulders to the hips, changing the ergonomics of mass and the moving body.

70. Merleau-Ponty, *The Phenomenology of Perception*.

71. In feminist theorist Karen Barad's agential realism the universe comprises phenomena of "intra-acting agencies" where objects emerge through particular intra-actions. From Barad's perspective, agency as a relationship, that is, not something a subject "has," but something which grows out of the intra-action between parts of the assemblage or apparatus, or in the case of clothing, between the body

and garment/prosthesis. (Barad, Karen (2007) *Meeting the Universe Halfway: Quantum Physics and the Entanglement of Matter and Meaning.* Durham: Duke University Press)

72. As noted by psychologist Silvan Tomkins, out social emotions are uniquely tied to the eyes and faces of others and we read the looks of others instinctively (even if expressions differ between cultures). As Tomkins points out, we are always aware of the eyes of others and by quick glances we seek to read their tone of emotion. This makes shame such powerful emotion, echoing deeply into the body as well as etching itself into emotive memory. As Tomkins writes,

> "Man is, of all animals, the most voyeuristic. He is more dependent on his visual sense than most animals, and his visual sense contributes more information than any of his senses." (Silvan Tomkins cited in Kosofsky Sedgwick & Frank (eds) *Shame and its sisters: a Silvan Tomkins reader,* Durham: Duke University Press, p.144)

Tomkins argue for emotions being hard-wired neurological responses, emerging in the very act of or prior to cognition. In Tomkins' work, shame and humiliation are our central affects as social animals and are often also the most intense, which also explains the continuous search for the gaze of our peers. (see also Kosofsky Sedgwick, Eve (2003) *Touching feeling: affect, pedagogy, performativity,* Durham: Duke University Press.)

73. Sartre uses the emotion of shame as a proof of the existence of the "other" the one who reveals me in a socially shameful situation, such as secretly peeping through a keyhole. (Sartre, Jean-Paul (1943/1969) *Being and nothingness: an essay on phenomenological ontology,* London: Routledge)

74. Today, social media "likes" takes these dynamics into another level, and our very self-image and its "identity" is a performative project where the subject continually needs to *achieve,* acclaim or a sense of progression. (Han, Byung-Chul (2015) *The burnout society,* Stanford: Stanford University Press)

75. Pfaller , Robert (2003) "Little Gestures of Disappearance: Interpassivity and the Theory of Ritual," *Journal of European Psychoanalysis,* Nr. 16, see also Zizek, Slavoj (1998) "The Interpassive Subject", Centre Georges Pompidou, Traverses, available at: http://www.lacan.com/zizek-pompidou.htm

76. Media theorist Felix Stalder argues cultures without commodities are the rebellious "coded" expressions of uncontrolled creativity, escaping institutions to form self-organized networks of DIY subcultures (as Dada and surrealist games, punkish DIY, zines etc), whereas commodities package codes into an easily digestible and sellable format – often turning a code of attitude into a mass-produced trend. (ex. punk became New Wave in the hands of the industry, a radical celebration of rebellion became a cult of the masquerade). (see Stalder, Felix (2005) *Open Cultures and the Nature of Networks,* Novi Sad: Kuda)

77. Maturana and Varela's focus on "languaging" could shift some of grounds in our understanding of how clothes are part of producing and manifesting identity: if clothes do not "mean" anything, but are about coordination of behaviors, it is not so much our thinking and reasoning that matters as much as what the body wants and desires. Clothes are vehicles for our being, not so much a poster-board for our abstract identity. Rather, from this perspective, the very ideas of an "identity" is an afterthought, an abstraction that tries to make sense of our behaviors. See Maturana, Humberto & Varela, Francisco (1987) *The tree of knowledge: the biological roots of human understanding*, Boston: Shambhala

78. "The Invisible Life of Clothes." *Invisibilia*. NPR, WNYC, 22 July. 2016.

79. An example of this may also be how the psychological atmosphere of certain work environments are also attuned to looks and behavior. Certain work environments attune the language, values and behaviours towards highly gendered stereotypes. Traditionally male environments, such as the army or truck drivers, may think, act and dress with a highly gendered attitude, and women introduced into such environments adopt masculine values and behaviors to blend into these cultures. Women soldiers "become" the attention and behavior of a soldier and may also alter their attitude towards traditionally feminine traits.

80. As suggested by psychologist Cameron Anderson and colleagues, we value local status, the admiration and respect of peers and face-to-face groups much more than relative macro status, that is, we don't seek the approval of distant idols, but from the peers who matter. (Anderson, C., Kraus, M. W., Galinsky, A. D., & Keltner, D. (2012) "The local-ladder effect: Social status and subjective well-being," *Psychological science*, 23(7), pp.764-771.)

81. This "programming" of how garments guide interactions and attentions resonates with sociologist Madeleine Akrich's notion of object's "script," which she defines, "like a film script, [by which] technical objects define a framework of action together with the actors and the space in which they are supposed to act." (Akrich, Madeleine (1992) "The de-scription of technical objects," Wiebe Bijker and John Law (eds) *Shaping technology/building society: studies in sociotechnical change*. Cambridge: MIT Press, p.208)

82. To Celia Lury, the technique of photography has also made us "see photographically," as it is a historically specific mode of cognition as well as a mnemonic technique that affects "configurations of self-and collective identity, experience and information." (Lury, Celia (1998) *Prosthetic culture: photography, memory, and identity*, London: Routledge, p.148) As a prosthetic culture, it makes us who we are, and who we think we are, shaping self-image and the stories we tell ourselves and others. Lury poses that through photographs, you extend yourself, and in doing so, gain control. "In adopting/adapting a prosthesis, the person creates (or is created by) a self-identity that is no longer defined by the edict 'I think, therefore I am'; rather he or she is constituted in the relation 'I can, therefore I am'"

83. In his book *The System of Objects* Baudrillard uses his invented brand GARAP as an example of how brands act as pure signification, without any content except the sign itself, and throughout this text we use Baudrillard's GARAP as an invented iconic brand, a brand of fashion as social dreaming, as Baudrillard puts it;

> 'Let us imagine for the moment modern cities stripped of all their signs, with walls bare like a guiltless conscience. And then GARAP appears. This single expression, GARAP, is inscribed on all the walls: pure signifier, without a signified, signifying itself. It is read, discussed, and interpreted to no end. Signified despite itself, it is consumed as sign. Then what does it signify, if not a society capable of generating such a sign? And yet despite its lack of significance it has mobilized a complete imaginary collectivity; it has become characteristic of the (w)hole of society. To some extent, people have come to '"believe" in GARAP.' (Baudrillard, Jean (1996) *The Systems of Objects*, London: Verso: p.198)

In correspondence with Baudrillard, an entry in the online Urban Dictionary notices that Garap denotes, "Something that's so spectacularly awesome and overwhelmingly epic that the commonly used words like "awesome" or "epic" fail to describe it."

84. In his discussion on the orientation of cognition, Damasio posits, "The orientation is only possible because feelings are integral to the cluster of operations that constitutes the sense of self, and because feelings are continuously generating, within the mind, a *concern* for the organism." (Damasio, *Looking for Spinoza: Joy, Sorrow and the Feeling Brain*, Orlando: Harcourt, p.208ff)

85. Ahmed, Sara (2006) *Queer phenomenology: orientations, objects, others*, Durham: Duke University Press.

86. This embodies approach differs from the class and culture-based perspective on "habitus" suggested by Bourdieu in his classic text *Distinctions* (1984) where he takes a more structural perspective on the development of distinctive tastes. Even if the outcomes may be similar (certain classes enjoy certain culture, music, food, drink etc) the emphasis here is on the cognitive feedback loops and emotional affirmations shared across a social group which manifest the orientations into aligning the peers' taste.

87. Like in Heidegger's example of the failed hammer, it is the event of failure that makes me feel the prosthesis in its fullest sense. (Heidegger, Martin (1927/2010) *Being and time*, Albany: State University of New York Press)

88. Masten, Carrie, Naomi Eisenberger, Larissa Borofsky, Jennifer Pfeifer, Kristin McNealy, John Mazziotta & Mirella Dapretto (2009) "Neural correlates of social exclusion during adolescence: understanding the distress of peer rejection," *Social Cognitive and Affective Neuroscience*, 4(2), pp. 143–157.

89. Lisa Blackman has written a very engaging work on the multiplicity of affects and voices within the self, or being "one yet many" while still mainly thinking of oneself as having one "personality," while most of us move through many emotional as well as embodied phases of life. With affect, our bodies are entangled into the environment and others, as pre-individual and trans-subjective and expanded (and multiple) selves. As Blackman suggests,

> "Rather than considering bodies as closed physiological and biological systems, bodies are open, participating in the flow or passage of affect, characterized more by reciprocity and co-participation than boundary and constraint" (Blackman, *Immaterial Bodies*, p.2)

As Blackman highlights, not even the immune system of the body draws a clear boundary of the body, autoimmune diseases breaks the boundary of body-as-fortress. When it comes to dress, this multiplicity of voices can also be seen in how we also dress to manifest who we are *not*, which may in turn encounter similar ambiguities as showing who we want to show we *are*, see Freitas, A., Kaiser, S., Joan Chandler, D., Carol Hall, D., Kim, J. W., & Hammidi, T. (1997) "Appearance Management as Border Construction: Least Favorite Clothing, Group Distancing, and Identity Not!" *Sociological Inquiry*, 67(3), pp.323-335.

90. Riva G. (2014) "Out of my real body: cognitive neuroscience meets eating disorders." *Front. Hum. Neurosci.* 8:236.

91. Kaiser argues for understanding style through social psychology, as a process which characterizes a visible identity constructions for individuals to articulate aesthetic as much as political social psychological desires - yearnings for belonging as well as liberation (Kaiser, Susan (1997) *The Social Psychology of Clothing: Symbolic Appearances in Context*, New York: Fairchild.) - Boultwood and Jerrard also examines this tension at the intersection between the body and style/fashion (Boultwood, Anne & Robert Jerrard (2000) "Ambivalence, and its relation to fashion and the body." *Fashion Theory*, 4.3, pp. 301-321.

92. Tseëlon, Efrat (1995) *The masque of femininity: the presentation of woman in everyday life*, London: Sage.

93. Damasio, *Looking for Spinoza*: p.96.

94. Damasio, *Looking for Spinoza*: p.40. Damasio's parallel to paramecium resonates well with Wilhelm Reich's argument how the protoplasm is the "morphological forerunner" of the human body and its functions are echoed in the human autonomic nervous system (Reich, Wilhelm (1982) *The bioelectrical investigation of sexuality and anxiety*, New York: Farrar, Straus and Giroux, p. 56).

95. Quartz and Asp differ between three pleasure machines in the brain; the Survival pleasure machine, the Habit pleasure machine and the Goal pleasure machine. Whereas the two first ones are basic to the sustainment of our lives in general, they

all race against each other, taking control at different times and contexts. (p. 24) The "social consumer," the consumer of cool as part of his or her status game, ties into our Goal systems of the brain, "that involves computing the expected utility of options in terms of their personal social valuation." (Quartz & Asp, *Cool*, p.250) - It is these last goal-pleasures we argue are activated through the gamble of fashion.

96. James, William (1890/1950) *The Principles of Psychology*, New York: Henry Holt.

97. James 1890/1950: p.292.

98. James 1890/1950: p.292.

99. Damasio, Antonio (2010) *Self comes to mind: Constructing the conscious brain.* New York: Pantheon Books.

100. It is important to notice that the importance of fashion phantom as an ideal self varies between people; those who seek no pleasure and have no interest in playing with fashion may also have less feedback from this type of mentalization of the self-image. It could relate to early experiences of gambling; those who get early reward find more pleasure in gambling, whereas those who lose the first couple of rounds learn that gambling is not for them (see Linden, *The compass of pleasure*, p.132ff). As a parallel to the gamble of social relations, mentalization also suggests the ability to understand the mind of another individual, especially framing their intentions, what philosopher Daniel Dennett calls the "intentional stance." The intentional stance highlights the ability to understand what others try to convey, even in contradictory forms of communication, such as metaphors and sarcasms. Yet, whereas empathy engages the emotions, that we feel the other person's feelings, metallization is more a question of understanding others. This in turn related to the "theory of mind" - that we in childhood gain the ability to relate to the mind in other beings (and thus we can be honest or lie to them etc) - Gamble, Clive, John Gowlett & Robin Dunbar (2014) *Thinking big: how the evolution of social life shaped the human mind*, London: Thames & Hudson, p.50f.

101. Eco, Umberto (1986) *Travels in hyperreality*, San Diego: Harcourt.

102. This perspective resonates well with the civilization process discussed by sociologist Norbert Elias, the internalized "self-restraint" imposed by increasingly complex social dynamics of shame and repugnance, working outward from a nucleus in court etiquette into bourgeois society, developing the repressive psychological self-perceptions that Freud recognized as the "super-ego." Following Elias, we come to experience social etiquette emotionally through processes of affirmation and rejection, thus anchoring social structures into the bodies of society (Elias, Norbert (1939/1994) *The civilizing process*, Oxford: Blackwell)

103. Social psychologist Barbara Fredrickson's study comparing the math performance of men and women dressed in sweaters or in a bathing suit famously confirms how wearers of bath suits become distracted from math performance, which

has become known as "objectification theory." The study suggests women are more likely than men to take on an "outsider" view their own appearance from "outside" or a third person perspective, thus objectifying themselves, which in turn negatively affects their performance. Fredrickson, B.L., Roberts, T.A., Noll, S.M., Quinn, D. M., & Twenge, J. M. (1998) "That swimsuit becomes you: Sex differences in self-objectification, restrained eating and math performance." *Journal of Personality and Social Psychology*, 75: pp.269-284.

104. Homeostasis, while it uses the word stasis, is perceived as a dynamic process for maintaining balance in yet that balance is never fully reached. Homeodynamics puts focus on how dynamic processes are used not to maintain a balance, but to induce and support continuous change - Steven Rose introduced the term homeodynamics in Rose, Steven (1998) *Lifelines: Biology Beyond Determinism*, Oxford: Oxford University Press, see also Lloyd, David, Miguel A. Aon, and Sonia Cortassa (2001) "Why homeodynamics, not homeostasis?." *The Scientific World Journal* 1, pp.133-145.

105. Riva, "Out of my real body."

106. Rochat, P. (2012) "Primordial sense of embodied self-unity," in V. Slaughter and C. Brownell (eds) *Early Development of Body Representations*, Cambridge: Cambridge University Press, pp.3–18.

107. As Damasio argues,

> "Now, where in the brain is that "feel-making" machinery? It is located in the brain stem and it enjoys a privileged situation. It is part of the brain, of course, but it is so closely interconnected with the body that it is best seen as *fused* with the body. I suspect that one reason why our thoughts are *felt* comes from that obligatory fusion of body and brain at brain stem level." (Damasio, Antonio (2010) "Self comes to mind," interview with Jonah Lehrer, *Wired/Science*, Nov 8, 2010)

108. Damasio differs between "images of the flesh" (nerves in muscles, flesh and the chemical parameters in the organism's interior) and "images from special sensory probes" (touch, vision, etc) (Damasio, *Looking for Spinoza*: 195ff), see also Damasio, Antonio (1999) *The Feeling of What Happens*)

109. Feelings reflect the state of the body in our brains, informing us that there is life inside the organism, letting us know it if it is in balance or not. That feeling is the foundation of the conscious mind. (Damasio, *The Feeling of What Happens*.)

110. Tsakiris, M., Longo, M. R., & Haggard, P. (2010) "Having a body versus moving your body: neural signatures of agency and body-ownership." *Neuropsychologia* 48, pp.2740–2749.

111. Sounds to auditory cortex, smells to olfactory cortex, visual inputs to occipital lobe. These pieces of information converge to the dorsal premotor cortex that ulti-

mately is recognized as the primary site where sense of limb position contributes to controlled movement.

112. The neural maps of the body also shifts the way we experience pleasure and pain, depending on context. While an "adrenaline rush" may limit our experience of pain, for example in a moment of stress, Damasio suggests our shift in perception is a "highly convenent modification of the current body maps. The modification requires several neural messages and does involve certain chemical molecules, although adrenaline probably is not the principal one. Soldiers in the battlefield also modify the body maps that portray pain and fear in their brains. Without that modification, acts of heroism would be less likely to occur. If this nice feature had not been added to the menu of our brains, evolution even might have discontinued childbirth in favor for a less painful variety of reproduction." (Damasio, *Looking for Spinoza*, p. 114.) We are thus more vulnerable in some situations and contexts, with highly sensitive maps active in the body, while other settings remake our maps to incorporate higher tolerance or shift the "focus" somewhere else. The neural maps are integrated in a part of the brain called the anterior insular cortex, every moment of our lives, to produce emotions and can be conceptualized as a serious of "global emotional moments" moving from the past to the anticipated future, in a self-aware stream of consciousness of cinemascopic "images." My phenomenal self emerges as we feel our bodies and identify these feelings as emerging from and belonging to our own bodies. (Di Lernia, Daniele et al. (2016) "Ghosts in the Machine. Interoceptive Modeling for Chronic Pain Treatment." *Frontiers in Neuroscience* 10: 314.)

113. Damasio, *Self comes to mind*, p.104.

114. We are conscious of our own body through experience of both its physicality— we perceive our body as a physical object in the external world—and it subjectivity—we experience our body through different neural representations that are not related to its physical appearance (Riva, "Out of my real body"). Without our conscious knowledge, information from proprioceptive neurons in our joints, visual input, tactile/haptic input, auditory inputs are integrated in associated areas, then perceived again as mapped "images" to actively create the experience of our bodies. In a famous study, when a rubber hand, placed in view of the subject, was stroked at the same as the real (hidden) hand, and only after a short time, subjects began to experience the rubber hand as if it was their own, and even mix up the location of their own hand at the end of the experiment: most subjects thought it was closer to the rubber hand than it was. (Botvinick, M & J Cohen (1998) "Rubber hands 'feel' touch that eyes see," *Nature* 391: 756) - In another experiment, researchers tricked participants into thinking they had three arms. They placed a prosthetic but realistic rubber arm next to a subject's right arm, then started touching both right arms with a brush in the corresponding locations, trying to make the two brushes identical in time and location, during which a conflict arises in the brain

concerning which of the right hands is experienced as one's own. This conflict is solved by accepting both right hands as part of the body image, and the subjects experience having an extra third arm. To test whether the arm had been incorporated, scientists threatened to cut off an arm with a knife and the person reacted with the same physiological response to both hands. - The dynamic nature of our physical bodies is apparent also in the case of phantom limbs, a phenomenon where a person with an amputated limb still feel the (often painful and mutated) experience of their limb. People claim to be able to use their imaginary limb to grasp objects. As people receive simultaneous and spatially accurate haptic and visual input, a seemingly stable and unchanging experience of our bodies is quick to shift. Our knowledge of the fact that the rubber hand is not attached to our bodies seems to have little impact over the experience of the simulated hand. In a very explicit way, experience seems to override reason when it comes to proprioception.

115. These are called episodic memories and are distinct from semantic memories (memories about impersonal facts such as remembering the capital of a foreign country).

116. Damasio, *The feeling of what happens*. - This is specific to the development of the temporal parietal cortex and the medial prefrontal cortex.

117. Damasio, Antonio (2010) *Self Comes to Mind*, New York: Pantheon Books, p.22. Damasio organizes the self slightly different and sees three ""stages of self. The first stage, the "protoself," is the primordial feeling of knowing that my body exists. The second stage, the "core self" is being aware of what happens, and feeling it: my organism has relationships to objects and events and I can act upon them. The third stage, the "auto-biographical self," is the feeling of knowing that I am me and is dependent on memory, that I know I have a past and a future, and how these memories tie into social and cultural relations.

118. Structurally, mPFC is able to process this type of complex interaction through reciprocal connections with brain regions that are implicated in emotional processing (amygdala), memory (hippocampus) and higher-order sensory regions (within temporal cortex) - Bateman, A., & Fonagy, P. (2010). "Mentalization based treatment for borderline personality disorder." *World Psychiatry*, 9 (1): 11–15.

119. Studies point to that people who have lost the ability to store and recall episodic memories cannot imagine themselves in the future. Also involved are hippocampal formation, PCC/precuneus (PCu), inferior parietal lobe, lateral temporal cortex. Spreng, R. Nathan, & Grady, Cheryl L. (2010) "Patterns of brain activity supporting autobiographical memory, prospection, and theory of mind, and their relationship to the default mode network," *Journal of Cognitive Neuroscience*, 22(6), pp.1112-23.

120. It is important to see that pretend play/inventing/crafting is about learning through imagining, then acting it out. But this is different from just imagining

without bodily action, which is what this area responsible for mentalization allows us to do. (Gopnik, Alison (2009) *The philosophical baby: what children's minds tell us about truth, love, and the meaning of life*, New York: Farrar, Straus and Giroux, also see, Gopnik, Alison & E. Seiver (2009) "Reading minds: How infants come to understand others." *Zero to Three*, 30(2), pp.28-32.

121. For the craftsman David Pye, it is the imaginal "resolution" when it comes to construction that differs the craftsman from the designer. For example, in making a new chair, the designer imagines all pieces fitting nicely together in his or her inner vision and drawing, but it is up to the craftsman to take on the nitty-gritty details of making the joints work and the pieces fit on a material level, which requires another type of practical visioning and creative imagination. (Pye, David (1968) *The nature and art of workmanship*, Cambridge: Cambridge University Press)

122. Entwistle, *The fashioned body*, p.7.

123. As Entwistle suggests;

> "Wearing the right clothes and looking our best, we feel at ease with our bodies, and the opposite is equally true: turning up for a situation inappropriately dressed, we feel awkward, out of place and vulnerable. In this respect, dress is both an intimate experience of the body and a public presentation of it. Operating on the boundary between self and other is the interface between the individual and the social world, the meeting place of the private and public." (Entwistle, *The fashioned body*, p.7.)

124. See for example Reich's work on the character - Reich, Wilhelm (1949) *Character analysis*, New York: Orgone Institute Press.

125. As noted by Quartz and Asp, under consumerism the use of clothes are central to the formation of selfhood in social relationships;

> "Just think of how your own pattern of consumption conveys who you are to yourself-and to others. For according to consumerism, without clothes your are more than naked. You are meaningless. This is because in a consumer culture things live a double life, both as material objects and as symbols and signals with meanings, both explicit and unrecognized, that communicate values, identities, aspirations, and even fears. All these add up to our lifestyles, made possible by consumerism." (Quartz & Asp, *Cool*, p. 5).

126. Mirror neurons were discovered in Macaque monkeys when scientists noticed that a specific group of neurons in an area of the brain involved with planning movements were active both when the animal performed a motor action and when they observed the same action executed by a human (Rostral part of the inferior premotor cortex)

127. Oughourlian, Jean-Michel (2016) *The Mimetic Brain*. East Lansing: Michigan State University Press: p.53.

128. Schoeck, Helmut (1969/1987) *Envy: a theory of social behaviour*, Indianapolis: Liberty Fund, but also Dumouchel, Paul (2014) *The Ambivalence of Scarcity and Other Essays*, East Lansing: Michigan State University Press.

129. Goffman, Erving (1959/1990) *The presentation of self in everyday life*, London: Penguin.

130. This may also help explain the sense of freedom, as well as anxiety, people feel as they break through social convention to "come out" and on purpose leave the safer realm of conformity. The experience of transgression is not limited to gender, but also appears in realms of ethnic, cultural or subcultural expressions. Perhaps the most mundane example is people buying certain clothes when on holiday to realize back home that the escapist self does not match the role back home. I may feel wonderful in my batik pants and dreadlocks during my month-long travel in Southeast Asia, only to realize back home in my conservative neighbourhood that I bounce back to my old self, just to feel secure. The "self" I found on my travels was too isolated and without peer-support when back home, a and I still find myself fettered to the opinion of my old peers.

131. Jones, S., and Yoshida, H. (2012) "Human bodies' goals and intentions," in V. Slaughter and C. Brownell (eds) *Early Development of Body Representations*, Cambridge: Cambridge University Press, pp.207–225.

132. Rochat, P. (2010) "The innate sense of the body develops to become a public affair by 2-3 years." *Neuropsychologia* 48, pp.738–745.

133. Rochat and Zahavi argue while commenting on the ideas formulated by Merleau-Ponty on mirror self-experience, underline: "…the decisive and unsettling impact of mirror self-recognition is not that I succeed in identifying the mirror image as myself. Rather, what is at stake here is the realization that I exist in an intersubjective space. I am exposed and visible to others. When seeing myself in the mirror, I am seeing myself as others see me. I am confronted with the appearance I present to others. In fact, not only am I seeing myself as others see me, I am also seeing myself as if I was an other, i.e., I am adopting an alienating perspective on myself… The me I see in the mirror is distant and yet close, it is felt as another, and yet as myself… I cannot freely establish a distance and perspective on it, as I can with other objects. Indeed, I cannot get rid of my exteriority, my exposed surface" (Rochat, P., and Zahavi, D. (2011) "The uncanny mirror: a re-framing of mirror self-experience." *Conscious. Cogn.* 20, p. 209).

134. Schilder, P. (1950) *The Image and Appearance of the Human Body*. New York: International UP, p.137 & 218.

135. As pointed out in the works of social psychologist Susan Fiske and her colleagues, status and emotions taint our cognitive processes, meaning that we sort people according to stereotypes pre-consciously, seemingly in the very act of per-

ception. (Fiske, S. T., Cuddy, A. J., Glick, P., & Xu, J. (2002) "A model of (often mixed) stereotype content: Competence and warmth respectively follow from perceived status and competition," *Journal of Personality and Social Psychology*, 82(6), pp.878–902.) As Fiske points out, prejudice becomes hardwired into our cognitive processes as we learn to sense the world, as does the emotion of envy (as well as the scorn of the people perceived as below us in the social hierarchies) - see Fiske, Susan (2011) *Envy up, scorn down: how status divides us*, New York: Russell Sage.

136. Indeed, friendship is a tricky phenomenon from a biological point of view, as we usually share little genetic history with friends. They start as strangers and possible threats, yet we manage to convert this animosity into alliances and trust. Friends may even be closer to us than our genetic relatives and we reveal things for them that we share with no other, and very few species develop them in ways similar to ours. (Silk, Joan B (2002) "Using the 'F'-word in primatology." *Behaviour*, 139.2-3 p.421.)

137. The trait we call "charismatic" in a person is usually a form of "social awareness" where the subject can feel the mood of an audience and reflect back their wishes of what that person should be. Clothes can help such endeavor as it may not only reflect a sense of belonging, but also give others attention through looks of approval and affirmation, thus "touching" their wishes and dreams.

138. MacLean, Paul. "Introduction" in Vogt, Brent Alan, and Michael Gabriel (1993) *Neurobiology of cingulate cortex and limbic thalamus*. Boston: Birkhäuser.

139. MacDonald, Geoff, and Mark R. Leary (2005) "Why does social exclusion hurt? The relationship between social and physical pain." *Psychological bulletin*, 131.2.

140. Eisenberger, et al, "Does rejection hurt?"

141. As pointed out by Chris Malone and Susan Fiske, the way we judge and hierarchize people around us ties into commodities too, such as products and brands. In relation to the unconscious prejudice that taints our cognition, also branding works to color products and brands with emotional values so that we sort our perception of them on an unconscious level. We start relating to corporations/ brands as another body (*corpus*), and "as customers, we perceive them as acting with intention and volition, just as we perceive other people." (Malone, Chris & Susan Fiske (2013) *The human brand: how we relate to people, products and companies*, San Francisco: Jossey-Bass, p.27.)

142. In anthropology there has been substantive discussions on the western-centric focus on understanding the individual as the basic building stone of culture, a concept which is not necessarily applicable across cultures, and might obscure relationships of mutualism, transactions, loyalty or a form of personhood deeply situated into its group. The importance of this turn is to acknowledge the fluid boundaries of personhood which leaves the contours of one's persona in a flux of

overlapping bonds, dependencies and alliances. In a parallel of cultural critique, Gerald Raunig's unpacking of the dividual emphasizes a more communal form of self, along a continuum between the atomist individual and the communal/homogenous (or between the individual-one and the all-one). The dividual is a personhood ties together with others, not cut off from them. As Raunig argues, it is a concept along the "conceptual line of the commune, the community, the common" attempting to escape the dogma of the identitarian individual (p.82) Rather than making the individual the foundational entity of the social realm (as favored by consumerism) Raunig argues a new sense of common-selfhood is needed to envision new futures away from separation, conflict and partition. (Raunig, Gerald (2016) *Dividuum: Machinic Capitalism and Molecular Revolution,* South Pasadena: Semiotext(e).)

143. Oughourlian, Jean-Michel (2016) *The Mimetic Brain.* East Lansing: Michigan State University Press, p. 33. Oughourlian's ideas, inspired by Rene Girard also overlaps well with the recent interest in the ideas of Gabriel Tarde of a sociology of desire (or affective sociology) as it puts emphasis on mimetic chains (or what Tarde calls "rays of imitation"), rather than the Freudian drives and emphasis on lack. See Trade, Gabriel (1899/2000) *Social laws: an outline of sociology,* Kitchener: Batoche, as well as, Trade, Gabriel (1903/2007) *The laws of imitation,* Ann Arbor: UMI.

144. Oughourlian differs between three different processes or "brains," and while Oughourlian's typology does not perfectly resonate with the three selves we have discussed earlier, it adds a dimension of interpersonal dynamics to the self which is important for understanding how fashion affects our sense of self through mimetics and social rivalry. The first brain is the cognitive and rational brain, it is the reasoning part where the subject forms cognitive functions, such as reason and judgement, and it is this type of brain Descartes activates in his famous statement that "I think, therefore I am." The second brain is the emotional or limbic brain, the center for emotional intelligence, or what American social theorist Jeremy Rifkin calls the "Homo empathicus." This is the social brain where we connect and see ourselves in others and learn to understand the benefits and costs of social bonds through emotions. Daniel Goleman suggests we have two "semi-independent" faculties or two minds, "one that thinks and one that feels." (Goleman, D (1995) *Emotional Intelligence,* New York: Bantam, p.10). The second brian also influences the first, as Goleman suggests two mnesiac systems, where facts become laden with emotions (such as joy, surprise, fear, anger, disgust etc), feelings (love, hate, resentment, envy, jealousy etc) and moods (good, bad, excited, depressed, slow or accelerated). As Oughourlian suggests, the limbic and emotional brain is also laden with a mirror system which explains "empathy and comprehension, transmission, contagion, and sharing of feelings, emotions and mood." (Oughourlian 2016: 53)

145. Damasio, Antonio (2005) *Descartes' error,* New York: Random House, p.100.

146. Damasio, *Descartes' error,* p. 240.

147. Oughourlian, *The mimetic brain,* p.56.

148. Oughourlian, *The mimetic brain,* p.59. It is worthy of notice that neuromarketing is far ahead in the understanding affective power and influence, whereas the academic fields still try to articulate what is happening. As media scholar Marie-Luise Angerer posits, it is as if the academics' desire *for* affect has over the last decade turned into a desire *after* affect - that affect has turned into what she calls a "dispositif of affect." (Angerer, Marie-Luise (2007/2015) *Desire after affect,* London: Rowman & Littlefield.

149. Oughourlian, *The mimetic brain,* p.59.

150. The inherent violent dynamics of mimesis is a central trope in Girard's "mimetic theory" - and also supported in other surveys, such as White, K., & Argo, J. J. (2011) "When Imitation doesn't flatter: The role of consumer distinctiveness in responses to mimicry." *Journal of Consumer Research,* 38, 667-680, a similar trope is Schoeck's work on the violence of envy. (Schoeck, Helmut (1969) *Envy: a theory of social behaviour,* New York: Harcourt)

151. Our desires are always imitated from others, that is now we come "in sync" with our friends and come to share emotional connections, interests and sympathize with each other. Similarly, we copy the behavior of peers, depending on how we see them act and in relation to their body type. For example, we see the size of a plate differently if we eat with thin people. (McFerran, B., Dahl, D. W., Fitzsimons, G. J., & Morales, A. C. (2010) "I'll have what she's having: Effects of social influence and body type on the food choices of others." *Journal of Consumer Research,* 36(6), pp.915-929.) We see ourselves in relation to others. This means there is always images of myself and others in my third brain, I continually mirror myself in the images of my peers and surroundings, and the context may also affect the emotional tone of this images of self and others. Yet our networked brains are not merely causal: we are not mirror images of our mimetic milieu (nor genetic clones of our parents). But as Oughourlian would have it, we are sucked into the forceful dynamics of our social environment, with its conflicts, rivalries and rewards.

152. Girard, René (1965) *Deceit, desire, and the novel: self and other in literary structure,* Baltimore: John Hopkins University Press. p.83

153. Oughourlian, *The mimetic brain,* p.7.

154. This aspect of self-formation is a central trope in the novels of Turkish author Orhan Pamuk, where the characters are always in obscure relations to their models or idols, always desiring to become the other. It is here Pamuk and Girard's image of the individual self is in alignments: I am always myself most when I become another. Childhood is nothing but a long process of learning to become oneself, and it never really stops: as a small child I try to act like my elder

sibling, I later challenge my friends in our games at the playground, I practice to walk like the model Iman, I imitate my boss and read management books sold at airports to become a better leader, imitating the most famous idols of our times, and most probably I will have a clue about which coffin I want to be buried in, having seen what style my idols were left in. Almost every aspect of myself is in continuous relationship to my peers and models and even if I retreat to become a solitary hermit on some lonely mountain, I most probably already have a conception of what that may be like in my mind. Indeed, there is a big chance some part of my mind will judge my efforts to become an hermit, saying I am not lonely enough or I should wear more ascetic looking sackcloth, surely in natural materials and earthen colors, to make my efforts more authentic. Being lonely in some stages of life gives me an emotional grounding to the experience of being a hermit, and I can thus strive for making that experience even more "authentic" by comparing it to how others have presented their withdrawal (also hermit life is a rivalry: how little can one eat, how long can one stay in a cave or on top of a pillar?)

155. Research show that wearers produce an self-objectifying image of themselves as they think of themselves primarily through appearance, (or as dressed.) This can be exemplified for example when users choose clothes for fashion over comfort, see Fredrickson, B. L., and Roberts, T. A. (1997) "Objectification Theory: toward understanding women's lived experience and mental health risks," *Psychol. Women Quarterly*, 21, pp.173–206, and for clothing especially, see Tiggemann, M., and Andrew, R. (2012) "Clothing choices, weight, and trait self-objectification." *Body Image*, 9, pp.409–412.

156. This ideal image can in some way resonate with Brian Massumi's idea of a "mirror-vision" (mirror-image) of the self, objectified through vision as an image (or mediated through photos) - a type of self-image Massumi differs from an affective "movement-vision" which is more in flux and animated through a flow of affects (Massumi, Brian (2002) *Parables for the Virtual: Movement, Affect, Sensation*, Durham: Duke University Press.) In our view, Massumi seems to limit the visual aspects of a mirror-vision to much to the ocular, that is seeing as restricting the image to only two dimensions, and discard that seeing is a form of touch and feeling. The latter aspect we would emphasise for the ideal: it is *an animated ideal we feel, and feel for.* For the connections to neuroscience and the ideal body, see Thompson, J. K. (1996) *Body Image, Eating Disorders and Obesity.* Washington, DC: APA - American Psychological Association, see also, Thompson, J. K., Heinberg, L. J., Altabe, M., and Tantleff-Dunn, S. (1999) *Exacting Beauty: Theory, Assessment and Treatment of Body Image Disturbance.* Washington, DC: American Psychological Association.

157. The importance of policing pleasure is a central trope in culture, as well as in fashion, and as highlighted by neuroscientist David Linden,

"Our legal systems, our religions, our educational systems are all deeply concerned with controlling pleasure. We have created detailed rules and customs surrounding sex, drugs, food, alcohol, and even gambling. Jails are bursting with people who have violated laws that proscribe certain forms of pleasure or who benefit by encouraging others to do so." (Linden, *The compass of pleasure*, New York: Penguin, p.3.)

158. Aron, Arthur, and Elaine N. Aron (1986) *Love and the expansion of self: Understanding attraction and satisfaction*. Hemisphere Publishing Corp/Harper & Row Publishers.

159. Ideals are shaped by cultural norms, yet marked somatically through experience. Thus the ideal-self as affected through fashion varies between contexts and cultures. This also relates to the pleasure of gambling for example, which is easily read as hedonist and in-productive, but as Linden suggests,

"the risk-taking, hard-driving, and obsessive personality traits often found in compulsive gamblers can be harnessed by some to make them very effective in the workplace. Many gambling addicts are amongst the most successful, productive, and innovative figures in the business world, a profile that contributes to a self-image of being in control and makes them extremely reluctant to seek help, even in dire circumstances." (Linden, The *compass of pleasure*, p.131.)

160. As British philosopher Simon Blackburn posits, the famous "Because I'm worth it" advert by L'Oreal reveals something deep about our quasi-elitist yet idealistic fascination with narcissism and praise of vanity,

"if occasionally [the models] looked pleasantly human, at least as often they seem to project self-absorption, or arrogance and disdain. They bestow the kind of smile that might be a sneer. They pout and sulk. Their vanity and indifference goes with being above us all, and perhaps knowing that they can call up our adulation and worship at will. The personae in the advertisements are simply out of reach. They do not care what we think of them. Like Narcissus, they appear to live in a world of their own, enclosed in their own self-love. Unsurprisingly, the models calculated to inflame our desires lure us with youth and beauty, and it is relatively easy to see that those are desirable features. We envy those who are handsome or beautiful, graceful, well-proportioned, symmetrical, glowing with youth and health." (Blackburn, Simon (2014) *Mirror, mirror: the uses and abuses of self-love*, Princeton: Princeton University Press, p.44f)

161. Bauman, Zygmunt (2007) *Consuming Life*, London: Polity, p.6.

162. As pointed out by Mark Wigley,

"A blurring of identity is produced by all prostheses. They do more than simply extend the body. Rather, they are introduced because the body is in some way 'deficient' or 'defective,' in Freud's terms, of 'insufficient,' in Le Corbusier's terms. In a strange way, the body depends on the foreign elements that transform it. It is reconstituted and propped up on the 'supporting limbs' that extend it. Indeed, it becomes a side effect of its extensions. The prosthesis reconstructs the body, transforming its limits, at once extending and convoluting its borders. The body itself becomes artifice." (Wigley, Mark (1991) "Prosthetic theory: the disciplining of architecture," *Assemblage*, 15, pp.7-29)

The ideal workings of the extended body also ties into competitive dynamics of identity production in the realm of dress and is well captured in Elizabeth Wissinger's (2015) *This year's model: fashion, media, and the making of glamour*, New York : New York University Press, but also on a societal scale in Byung-Chul Han (2015) *The burnout society*, Stanford: Stanford University Press.

163. Coming back to Adam and Galisky's ideas of "enclothed cognition," we can feel our different sense of self clash where things "fit together" or another sense of self becomes "too much" - or we may feel exactly dressed right as these various aspects of ourselves come together perfectly and it all "feels right." In Adam and Galisky's example, the doctor wearing the doctor's coat enhances the ideal self, whereas recognizing that the what the doctor thought was his or her coat was a painter's coat undermines this ideal sense of self. The example tells us how we cannot fully be "ourselves" if we are not dressed to the occasion. The dressed realm acts on many levels, and we would argue most is expressed in subtle micro-signals: silences, side looks, nods, whispers, signals we hardly recognize, but which leave emotional traces. We can often "read" the atmosphere of a group in a room without speaking to anyone, or we sense the disquiet mood of a friend by a special type of silence or faint expression. Yet we feel how others reacts, we sense those subtle looks which express "too much" or "too revealing" or "wrong shoes" - the quick movements of eyes, the smirks, the small small social signals which confirm or refuse our dressed social aspirations, and since fashion is "shallow" we also lack a vocabulary to pinpoint these feelings we are not supposed to feel (being told that "it's the inside that counts" is not really much comfort). Our emotional attention to ambience and atmosphere is often used in marketing. In a famous study researchers found consumers buying more expensive wines when the wine store played classic music rather than a playlist of top-40 hits. (Areni, Charles S. and David Kim (1993) "The Influence of Background Music on Shopping Behavior: Classical Versus Top-Forty Music in a Wine Store", in *NA - Advances in Consumer Research*, Volume 20, Leigh McAlister and Michael L. Rothschild (eds), Provo, UT: Association for Consumer Research, pp: 336-340.)

164. Mike Featherstone opens a very fruitful discussion on the animation of the self-image through affect in consumer culture. He argues that synesthesia ("the way the senses work together to produce not only our perception of the world, but the way we sense other bodies when we encounter then in everyday life, or through

various media") can be a way to move away from the ocularcentric ideas concerning what we conceive as the image in a "self-image." Following Massumi, Featherstone argues for a distinction between a body sees a commodity-driven mirror-image (the instrumental self we can transform through consumerism, training, plastic surgery etc) and a body-without-image which is the more open and process-oriented as well as affective body-schema (p.195f). Featherstone writes,

> "While the body without image, the affective body can be represented as an opposite to the body image in the visual 'mirror-image' mode, the distant goal of the consumer culture transformative process is to bring both together - the power to affect others, through the beautification process and the enhancement of 'the look' coupled with an appropriate body style of presentation." (p.196)

Featherstone calls this type of a photographic self-image an ideal *imago*, imago as a projected persona, a fantasmatic model of the self held in 'the mind's eye' - a model of what one should or could be.

> "Clothes, make-up and adornment are important here. They are not just the exterior signs, the constructed appearance of what one wants others to see, but also reflexively they provide ab outward image which seeks confirmation in the returned glances of others, for the inner narrative of what one feels one should be. This is the made-up person, living out, or actualizing a particular temporary fiction, or moving through the life course to realize a particular larger narrative." (p.198)

While the typology of Featherstone does not directly overlap with ours, and we would argue that our transformative mirror-image (or imago) is deeply connected to our body-schema, we would suggest the fashion phantom is somewhat of the amalgamation of the two modes: an ideal projection with strong somatic markers. (Featherstone, Mike (2010) "Body, Image and Affect in Consumer Culture, *Body & Society*, 16.1, pp.193-221.)

165. As we see it, the ideal-self is a tool that connects us to our desires rather than being a thing in-between them: it is an amalgamation of ideal images, how we project our selves through desires, as felt in the body.

166. As in cognition "having a world" - as we are all dressed the phantasma of fashion is a cognitive world for us, it is a world we "have" (and not only "see"): we *are in it, and of it.* (see Varela & Dupuy, *Understanding Origins*).

167. It is important to notice that the social imagination is part of an aesthetic Zeitgeist: the current collective desires and looks of aspiration (the Zeitgeist as a time-specific imaginal realm). As a parallel, it is interesting that the idea of a Zeitgeist ties into Thomas Carlyle's hero-worship exemplified in his argument that the history of the world is but the biography of great men (and the hero as a divinity in special resonance with the Zeitgeist). Also fashion is a worship of aesthetic he-

roes, artists with a special connection to the time, worthy of worship through quasi-divine rituals, (as in Carlyle's voice of Diogenes Teufelsdröckh in *Sartor Resartus.*)

168. Spinoza, *Ethics*, part 3, prop. 6. - As Deleuze has it, *conatus* "is the effort to experience joy, to increase the power of acting, to imagine and find that which is a cause of joy, which maintains and furthers this cause; and also an effort to avert sadness, to imagine and find that which destroys the cause of sadness" (Deleuze, Gilles (1970/1988) *Spinoza: Practical Philosophy*, San Francisco: City Lights: p.101)

169. This plasticity of both body and mind on a neurological level makes the living being more adaptable than previously thought, making the interface between the environment and organism highly malleable and transformative. The interaction between world and body where bodies are shaped, used, performed and ornamented, is highlighted by professor Tobin Siebers in his groundbreaking contribution to disability studies where he argues that "The body is alive, which means that it is as capable of influencing and transforming social languages as they are capable of influencing and transforming it." (Siebers, Tobin (2008) *Disability Theory*, Ann Arbor: University of Michigan press: p.68)

170. The Baltic German biologist Jakob von Uexküll phrased the term "Umwelt" to pinpoint how every organism has a specially attuned sensory environment, or a "self-centered world." According to Uexküll different organisms have different umwelten, even though they share the same physical environment. For example, a world for a dog is more richly defined by the olfactory senses and markers than a human environment, which instead is richer in visual signs. The signifying form of the Umwelt creates what biosemioticians call a "semiosphere," a world of biological signifiers which guide encounters and interactions between organisms and environments (von Uexküll, Jakob (1934/2010) *A foray into the worlds of animals and humans*, Minneapolis: University of Minnesota Press). Parallels can also be drawn to Dawkins' ideas of the "extended phenotype," how organisms build extensions of their bodies as part of their being: for example the anthills of the ants. Similarly, humans use clothes as an extension of the phenotype. (Dawkins, Richard (1982) *The extended phenotype: the gene as the unit of selection*, Oxford: Freeman).

171. According to Quartz and Asp, brands are ubiquitous as they act in correspondence to our Habit pleasure machine: a brand is a way of making sense of the world and activate brain regions of memory, emotion and recollection, modulating our sensory experience - or the whole field of emotional branding with its center at how *expectations shape experience*. (Quartz & Asp, *Cool*, p.55f)

172. Crawford discusses the shift in perspective on phantom limbs as follows, "Phantoms have undeniably been at times ethereal, embodied traces characterized by inauthenticity and devoid of an essential ontology. But, they have also unequivocally been objects invested with social substance and with material integrity. Through-

out their history, eternal limbs have been for some researchers and practitioners the Holy Grail of neuroscience, sacred objects with miraculous powers. For others, they have been pure vacuousness, mere vestiges, or worthless psychic baggage." (Crawford, *Phantom limb*, p.19)

173. Ramachandran, Vilanur & Sandra Blakeslee (1999) *Phantoms in the brain: human nature and the architecture of the mind*, London: Fourth Estate

174. Ramachandran & Blakeslee, *Phantoms in the brain*, p.35.

175. Crawford writes,

> "Phantoms remake the morphology of human bodies—sometimes in bizarre and very distorted ways—and they remap the geography of human codices, effectively disturbing what was once considered immutable. Phantoms are imbued with social substance and material integrity because they are at once work objects and actants." (Crawford, *Phantom limb*, p.149).

This makes Crawford identify the link between phantoms and prosthetics in correspondence with Karen Barad's "agential realism" where the "material-discursive" nature of a "world [that] kicks back." Barad, Karen (1999) "Agential realism: Feminist interventions in understanding scientific practices." In Biagioli (ed) *The science studies reader*, New York: Routledge, p.3, cited in Crawford, *Phantom limb*, p.152.

176. Ramachandran & Blakeslee, *Phantoms in the brain*, p.58.

177. First defines the disorder as "an unusual dysfunction in the development of one's fundamental sense of anatomical (body) identity." (First, M. B. (2005). "Desire for amputation of a limb: paraphilia, psychosis, or a new type of identity disorder." Psychol. Med. 35, p.919 see also Brugger, Peter, Bigna Lenggenhager, and Melita J. Giummarra (2013) "Xenomelia: a social neuroscience view of altered bodily self-consciousness." *Frontiers in psychology* 4: 204, and McGeoch, P. D., Brang, D., Song, T., Lee, R. R., Huang, M., and Ramachandran, V. S. (2011) "Xenomelia: a new right parietal lobe syndrome." *Journal of Neurology, Neurosurgery & Psychiatry*, 82, pp.1314–1319.

178. Case, Laura Kristen (2013) *How the Body Can Feel Wrong: Sensory Processing and Neural Body Representation in Transsexuality and Anorexia Nervosa*, Dissertation, University of California, San Diego.

179. Ammenheuser, Maura (2016) "'Phantom fat': When you still feel oversized even after losing weight," *MySouthernHealth*, February 23, 2016.

180. Phillips, Katharine (2004) "Body dysmorphic disorder: recognizing and treating imagined ugliness," *World Psychiatry*. 2004 Feb; 3(1), pp.12–17.

181. Grant, J. E. & Phillips, K. A. (2004) "Is anorexia nervosa a subtype of body dysmorphic disorder? Probably not, but read on…" *Harvard Review of Psychiatry*, 12(2), pp.123-126.

182. Macsween, Morag (1993) *Anorexic Bodies: A Feminist and Sociological Perspective on Anorexia Nervosa*, London: Routledge.

183. Buhlmann, U., Teachman, B. A., Naumann, E., Fehlinger, T., & Rief, W. (2009) "The meaning of beauty: Implicit and explicit self-esteem and attractiveness beliefs in body dysmorphic disorder." *Journal of Anxiety Disorders*, 23(5), pp.694-702.

184. Phillips, Katharine (2005) *The Broken Mirror: Understanding and Treating Body Dysmorphic Disorder*, Oxford: Oxford University Press, p.191.

185. With their focus on transformation, fashion ties the body seamlessly into modernity and consumer culture, centering on individual self-invention and self-design. (Giddens, Anthony (1991) *Modernity and self-identity*, Oxford: Polity.) This in turn, as modelled through the -68 counterculture movement becomes paired into a mode of freedom, quickly appropriated by marketing. The corruption of this kind of freedom into advertising, consumerism and political control can be followed in the British television documentary series "The Century of the Self" (2002) by filmmaker Adam Curtis.

186. Throughout all these stages, we shape emotionally laden images of ourselves and our clothes, what worked well, what got rejected, what drew good attention and what not, etching emotions deep into the body-schema and auto-biographical self, but also higher up in consciousness where we start to know what works and in what settings. Depending on the feedback signals we get from our surroundings, we get a "feel" for what works and not within that specific community. However, as time and social groupings move on, so does our ideal self, and the fashion phantom moves along with the zeitgeist; and so does the position of the fashion phantom in relation to the evolving popular styles. Some people get a sense of what is coming into trend and how to relate to it, or how to position themselves in a scene using clothes and other signals for what earns a position within the group: read the latest books, listen to the new music, follow the sport seasons or keeping in tune with fashion. The new is a frontier which we use to "tune in" with our social networks and the boundaries for what works and does not work gives shape to the fashion phantom. - This resonates somewhat with W. H. Auden observation, that, "Young people, who are still uncertain of their identity, often try on a succession of masks in the hope of finding the one which suits them — the one, in fact, which is not a mask." (W. H. Auden, "One of the Family", in *Forewords and Afterwords*, London: Faber & Faber, 1973, p.369.)

187. Many of us have vivid (and perhaps uncomforable) memories of our clothing in teenage years, not unlike how how we remember the lyrics to songs we liked at that age. As an interesting parallel, Daniel Levitin points that music from our early teens often becomes "our" music. Even patients with Alzheimer and profound memory loss can still remember how to sing songs from their early teens.

> "Particularly when we are young, and in search of our identity, we form bonds or social groups with people whom we want to be like, or whom we believe we have something in common with. As a way of externalizing the bond, we dress alike, share activities, and listen to the same music. Our group listens to this kind of music, those people listen to that kind of music. This ties into the evolutionary idea of music as a vehicle for social bonding and social cohesion. Music and musical preferences become a mark of personal and group identity and of distinction." (p.232)

And Levitin connects this overlap of emotional and social bonding to the development of our brain,

> "Part of the reason we remember songs from our teenage years is because those years were times of self-discovery, and as a consequence, they were emotionally charged; in general, we tend to remember things that have an emotional component because our amygdala and neurotransmitters act in concert to 'tag' the memories as something important. Part of the reason also has to do with neural maturation and pruning; it is around fourteen that the wiring of our musical brains is approaching adultlike levels of completion." (Levitin, *This is your brain on music*, p.232)

188. Levitin also suggests the possibility of mirror neurons firing in the social settings of engaging with music, that the social element of seeing music being performed reaches "deeper" into our cognition (Levitin, *This is your brain on music*, p.267)

189. Based on the parity principle as posited by philosopher Andy Clark, when something plays a role that would be considered a cognitive process if it happened inside our brains, it is playing a role in our cognition. it is an extension of our cognition. So clothes, we argue, are an extension of our cognition. Clark, Andy, and David J. Chalmers (2010) "The Extended Mind," in Richard Menary, (ed.) *The Extended Mind*, Cambridge: MIT Press: pp.26-42.

190. Plato (Theaetetus 152c)

191. Aristotle (De Anima 432a)

192. Bottici, Chiara (2014) *Imaginal politics: images beyond imagination and the imaginary*, New York: Columbia University Press, p.18.

193. Aristotle (De Anima 433b 29)

194. As Bottici sees it, the imaginal is a category that points beyond the impasse of a choice between theories of the imagination as an individual faculty and theories of the imaginary as a social context, and thus the imaginal can be both conscious and unconscious, social and individual. The concept of the imaginal differs from that of imaginative, which either denotes a person's individual faculty of imagination or system of pre-programmed imagination. The term *imaginal* is also used by Henry

Corbin and Cynthia Fleury, who derive it from Sufi origin and medieval Iranian metaphysician Sohravardi. Philosophers such as Walter Benjamin and Henri Bergson trace similar ideas in the debate between realism and idealism by high-lighting the way images have a materiality.

195. We thus align body posture and experience with inner models of what certain experiences "should" feel like, or how we have imagined them beforehand, and thus adopt perception to pre-conceived mental models. Neuroscientist Vilayanur Ram-achandran argues for a similar stance when it comes to perception and our experi-ence of reality when he posits "the line between perceiving and hallucinating is not as crisp as we like to think. In a sense, when we look at the world, we are halluci-nating all the time. One could almost regard perception as the act of choosing the one illumination that best fits the incoming data. which is often fragmentary and fleeting." (Ramachandran, V.S. (2011) *The Tell-Tale Brain: A Neuroscientist's Quest for What Makes Us Human*, London: W.W.Norton, p.229).

196. Many studies on the ideal body emphasises how the manipulation of images in various forms of media are in many ways distorting and polluting our ideals. For example, Susan Bordo's important work highlights how we rarely see an media images of unaltered faces and bodies (and today unfiltered social media posts) - something she argues shapes our standard of judgment and enhances a continuous sense of inadequacy. While such images may affect our ideal selves and self-image, we want to put more emphasis on the mimetic peer-dynamics, rather than a collec-tive unconscious of media images. The fashion phantom moves through ideals for sure affected by media, but the bodily interactions and glances which affirm our sense of affirmation comes from peers and the imagination and attention we share. (Bordo, Susan (1993) *Unbearable Weight: Feminism, Western Culture, and the Body*, Berkeley: University of California Press.)

197. As noted by Sarah Jain, a the consumerist notion of body amplification repro-duces a continuous need and a planned anxiety within dissatisfied consumers. A "prosthesis falters between two renditions of meaning; a prosthesis can fill a gap, but it can also diminish the body and create a need for itself." (p.44) Many abstract concepts are manifested through prosthetic needs, "as in the case of cigarettes, the inherent dangers of the products have been conscientiously disclaimed in the overt sexualization of the products in marketing strategies that entwine the product with the identity and potency of the owner and, ultimately, with a version of free-dom itself." (p. 45) As Jain further suggests, a consumer version of a missing phan-tom limb is produced as "marketing attempts to evoke a certain nostalgia in the consumer in a promise for a 'complete' body." (p. 45) Jain also stresses, how the prosthesis also provokes insufficient cultivated sympathy or pity; "Raced bodies, aged bodies, gendered bodies are always already not whole enough and require more subtle tools than those that can be squeezed out of the term 'prosthesis' in its many incarnations." (p. 48) - see Jain, Sarah (1999) "The prosthetic imagination:

Enabling and disabling the prosthesis trope," *Science, Technology, & Human Values,* 24:1, pp.31-54.

198. Mandel, Naomi, Derek D. Rucker, Jonathan Levav, Adam D. Galinsky (2017) "The Compensatory Consumer Behavior Model: How Self-Discrepancies Drive Consumer Behavior" *Journal of Consumer Psychology.* January 2017, Vol. 27, Issue 1, pp.133-146.

199. Bauman, Zygmunt. "Perpetuum mobile." *Critical Studies in Fashion & Beauty* 1.1 (2010): pp.55-63. A parallel to this tension can be found in Eve Kosofsky Sedgwick's analysis of an advertisement campaign by cigarette manufacturers on smoker's rights as a form of human rights;

> "I see these ads as the warning taunt of a blackmailer, aimed at smokers, at driving ever in and against then the ugly twisting point that in the present discursive constructions of consumer capitalism the powers of our 'free will' are always already vitiated by the 'truth' of compulsion, while the powers attaching to an acknowledged compulsion are always already vitiated by the 'truth' of our free will." (Sedgwick, Eve Kosofsky (1992) "Epidemics of the will," in Jonathan Crary & Sanford Kwinter (eds) *Incorporations,* New York: Zone. pp.582-595.)

200. Bauman, "Perpetuum mobile," p.59.

201. Bauman, "Perpetuum mobile," p.60.

202. Bauman, "Perpetuum mobile," p.61.

203. As sociologist Robert Faris argues, popular and well-connected people may have a "connective status" but this does not make the person part of the elite. Instead, to earn elite status a subject must have "bridging status", that is, offer connections through social barriers and keeps these connections open only to a selected few. For such connections to remain of value, they must be defended against intrusion and value inflation, and thus the elite must strive to uphold networks through "reputational aggression" (Faris, Robert (2012) "Aggression, exclusivity, and status attainment in interpersonal networks." *Social Forces* 90(4), pp.1207-1235)

204. Ramachandran & Blakeslee, *Phantoms in the brain.*

205. For example, Melzack describes how one of his patients suffered pain as a consequence of his inability to stop his phantom legs from cycling continuously. The spasms of the phantom arm and hand can be so real and powerful that she avoided close contact with other people and objects because of the fear of hitting them. (Melzack, R. (1989). Phantom limbs, the self and the brain (the D. O. Hebb Memorial Lecture). *Canadian Psychology/Psychologie canadienne, 30*(1), pp.1-16.). - see also Crawford, *Phantom limb,* p.46f.

206. Acute pain fulfills an informative need aimed at the avoidance of organic damage, but chronic pain serves no purpose for an organism. Di Lernia et al suggest that people with chronic pain conditions live with a residual interoceptive image, or ghost, of chronic pain that results from the strength and precision of past sensation that floods our interoceptive senses instead of learning from and changing through dynamic interactions with our internal and external environments. This overflow produces a "diminished interoceptive precision" which fails to adapt to new conditions, thus prolonging pain sensations indefinitely. (Di Lernia D, Serino S, Cipresso P and Riva G (2016) "Ghosts in the Machine. Interoceptive Modeling for Chronic Pain Treatment." *Frontiers in Neuroscience* 10:314.)

207. The feminine body is traditionally regarded a sexual body and an embodiment of sexual reproduction and thus culturally controlled. Even in times of greater gender equality "women are still seen as located in the body" Entwistle argues, "whereas men are seen as transcending it. Thus, while a woman can wear a tailored suit much the same as a man's, her identity will always be that of a 'female professional', her body, her gender being outside the norm 'masculine'". As Entwistle points out, men and women are embodied culturally in different ways and the cultural associations of their embodiment differs. (Entwistle 2015: 38) Throughout this book we will try to give an overview of emotional embodiment and draw examples from both masculine and feminine experiences.

208. Annett, Kate (2015) "Do Fashion Trends Still Exist?", *Business of Fashion*, January 9, 2015, available at: https://www.businessoffashion.com/articles/intelligence/fashion-trends-still-exist - yet it is important to notice that the end of fashion has been spelled out for a long time by now, not least after bestsellers like Teri Agins' (2000) *The end of fashion: how marketing changed the clothing business forever,* New York: Quill and Dana Thomas' (2007) *Deluxe: how luxury lost its luster,* New York: Penguin Press.

209. Lee, Michele (2003) *Fashion Victim: Our Love-Hate Relationship with Dressing, Shopping, and the Cost of Style,* New York: Broadway Books

210. This phenomenon resonates with what fashion scholar Efrat Tseelon calls "semiotic fatigue" where layers of meaning, irony and play with symbols dissolves signification in a maelstrom of simulations. (Tseëlon, Efrat (2015) "Jean Baudrillard: post-modern fashion as the end of meaning." in Rocamora & Smelik (eds) *Thinking Through Fashion: A Guide to Key Theorists,* London: I.B. Tauris: p.225

211. see, for example; Lanier, Jaron (2010) *You are not a gadget: a manifesto,* New York: Knopf, and Lanier, Jaron (2018) *Ten arguments for deleting your social media accounts right now,* London: Random House.